LOT (QUERCY)

£1.50 (8)
Apr

Arthur Eperon is one of the most experienced and best-known travel writers in Europe. Since leaving the RAF in 1945 he has worked as a journalist in various capacities, often involving travel. He has concentrated on travel writing for the past twenty-five years and contributed to many publications including *The Times*, *Daily Telegraph*, *New York Times*, *Woman's Own*, *Popular Motoring* and the *TV Times*. He has also appeared on radio and television and for five years was closely involved in Thames Television's programme *Wish You Were Here*. He has been wine writer to the RAC publications and a number of magazines.

He has an intimate and extensive knowledge of France and its food and wine as a result of innumerable visits there over the last forty years. In 1974 he won the *Prix des Provinces de France*, the annual French award for travel writing.

Also available in Eperon French Regional Guide series:

NORMANDY

BRITTANY

EPERON'S FRENCH REGIONAL GUIDES

LOT (QUERCY)

ARTHUR EPERON

PAN BOOKS
LONDON, SYDNEY AND AUCKLAND

First published 1990 by Pan Books Ltd
Cavaye Place, London SW10 9PG
9 8 7 6 5 4 3 2
© Arthur Eperon 1990
Illustrations © Mary Fraser 1989
Maps © Ken Smith 1989

Designed by Peter Ward

ISBN 0 330 31220 0

Photoset by Parker Typesetting Service, Leicester
Printed in England by Clays Ltd, St Ives plc

This book is sold subject to the condition that it
shall not, by way of trade or otherwise, be lent, re-sold,
hired out, or otherwise circulated without the publisher's prior
consent in any form of binding or cover other than that in which
it is published and without a similar condition including this
condition being imposed on the subsequent purchaser

CONTENTS

KEY TO PRICES

MEALS		ROOMS	
	A = Under 75F		A = Under 100F
	B = 75–90F		B = 100–150F
	C = 90–125F		C = 150–200F
	D = 125–150F		D = 200–250F
	E = 150–175F		E = 250–350F
	F = 175–225F		F = 350–450F
	G = over 225F		G = over 450F

Room prices per night for double room without breakfast.
Meals include tax and service.

1 *Departments of France*

INTRODUCTION

To most people, even to most Frenchmen, the Lot means a river as beautiful as the Dordogne, flowing through fertile fields and bare, wild rock. Tell them that the 'Lot' means also quiet beautiful farmlands, great lonely sheep pastures, and many rivers running through deep ravines with few people and fewer industries and they will probably look puzzled. Show them on the map and the French at least will say: 'Ah – Quercy!'

For the French have not taken to these new-fangled names of Lot and Dordogne for their départements. To them these départements are still called Quercy, Périgord and Limousin.

The two ancient regions of Haut-Quercy and Bas-Quercy were united into a département called Lot after the Revolution. Then in 1808 Napoleon changed all that by taking away much of Bas-Quercy and forming it into a second département called

Villeneuve-sur-Lot

Tarn-et-Garonne with parts of Gascony, Languedoc and Rouergue added. So it is inevitable that in this book I have wandered beyond Lot, for travellers do not stop at local government boundaries. If you are driving west from Cahors along the lovely Lot valley you are almost certain to continue among the rich fruit and vegetable farms around Villeneuve-sur-Lot where they grow asparagus, artichokes, peas and tomatoes, melons, peaches, pears, apples, cherries and especially plums. Then you may make for Agen, on the river Garonne, where the plums are dried to become the world renowned Agen prunes. Now you are in Lot-et-Garonne département.

Similarly, if you drive south from Cahors on N20 the beautiful scenery continues way past Montpezat-de-Quercy as far as the important market town of Montauban on the Tarn river. Napoleon may have called it Tarn-et-Garonne and Paris bureaucrats do today, but the people of the south-west call it Quercy, as their ancestors did.

So I have taken the liberty of interpreting the area called Lot very liberally and unbureaucratically by calling the book Lot and Quercy and including the départements of Lot, Tarn-et-Garonne and Lot-et-Garonne. I hope that the powers in Paris will forgive me.

We British are so accustomed to calling the whole area both sides of the Dordogne river from Bergerac to Castelnau 'the Dordogne' that it comes as a surprise to find that the busy town of Souillac, the delightful market town of St Céré, the caves of Lacave and Padirac and even the most spectacular of mediaeval cities, Rocamadour, are actually in Lot. So is Martel, which is north of the Dordogne river.

All this belongs, by any standards, in a guide to Lot and happens to be one of my favourite hide-out areas in all France – beautiful, quiet but not dull.

This is the area called Haut-Quercy, with two great plains called the Martel Causse and Gramat Causse. Here you will see sheep grazing on rather dry pastures divided by dry stone-dykes, with vineyards and some other crops in the valleys below.

A lot of tobacco was grown until recently but is being replaced by soft fruit, although you can still see tobacco hung up to dry in the sun. The Gramat Causse, which has an average

Vallée du Lot

height of 350 metres is broken by mighty canyons, like huge gashes, cut by the rivers Ouysse, Alzou and Cère, tributaries of the Dordogne. It is spectacular scenery, with grand horizons.

You will find many old Quercy houses in Haut-Quercy. Their roofs are of flat stones or tiles and they have outside stone staircases leading to the first floor, where the family lives. Below on the ground floor is a large room or cellar used as a sheep shelter or for storing machinery and crops. Beside the houses or nearby on the farm you can still find old dovecotes raised on brick stilts. Once pigeons were not only kept for food but also for manure, and the pile of droppings under the dovecote was so important that its value was assessed when farms were sold or split among inheriting children.

The Limogne Causse south of Cahors in Bas-Quercy has

long narrow ridges on which sheep graze and oak trees flourish in the clay soil. Lalbenque, south-east of Cahors, is almost as famed as Sarlat and Périgueux in the Dordogne for truffles, those elusive underground mushrooms which hide beneath truffle oaks to be snuffled out by trained dogs and sold at prices beyond most people's reach to add an elusive flavour to pâtés, sauces and even simple omelettes. Dogs are preferred to pigs as truffle-hounds these days. The pigs used to eat too many before the farmers could stop them. And you can carry a dog on a bicycle or moped.

The valleys of Bas-Quercy are rich and fertile. Fields bordered by poplars to protect from wind or fierce summer sun produce fruit, vines and cereals.

It is the valleys of the Lot and Célé, too, which provide the best living for the people of the villages and small towns and which lure travellers because of their spectacular beauty. The Lot winds and meanders as snakily as the Dordogne and in many places you can stand above it on a bank or clifftop and see beautiful and spectacular views. One of the finest is from the esplanade outside the town hall of Puy l'Évêque, just west of Cahors and in the very heart of the Cahors wine country. At Cahors and Luzech the river loop almost forms a circle, so canals and dams were built to try to straighten it. The Célé feeds the Lot, which continues westward to join the Garonne, so it was

Truffle hunting of old

once important for navigation. Barges called *sapines* and *gabares* carried Auvergne cheese and Cahors wine to Bordeaux. Most of the wine went to England. As in Dordogne, many old castles look down on the river. They were built for war, unlike the Loire castles which were built for love and fêtes.

Visitors have begun to drift southward to Lot from the Dordogne. You will not find so many green and idyllic hideaways nor such lush and beautiful greenery but you will find many attractive little villages, tiny roads used almost entirely by farmers and far, far fewer visitors and their cars. Away from the tourist sites of Rocamadour, Souillac and Padirac, Lot is as undiscovered as Dordogne of 40 years ago. And although you can find holiday *gîtes*, they are nothing like so frequent as in Dordogne.

Quercy has been a poor area for centuries. In the 1800s villages became almost destitute. Poverty continued until recent times. People moved away from the countryside into the growing industrial cities of the north until a few years ago. Farms grew uneconomically small because of French inheritance laws dividing property among all children. With the post-war boom in cities and new factories and the Gaullist policy of discouraging farms too small to be mechanised or modernised, so many of the young people from Dordogne and Lot moved away that the population dropped to below what it was two hundred years ago. Cottages were abandoned, so were less lucrative vineyards. More recently French Government aid to people buying and modernising houses has enticed people to buy them as second homes, holiday cottages to let or for future retirement. Some buyers have come from Holland, Belgium and Britain, but there has been nothing like the rush that took place in the Dordogne. An astute Parisian businessman told us recently that the countryside south of Souillac was one of the best areas to find a bargain in country cottages for modernisation.

Certainly in the small roads south of Souillac and Cahors you can still get comprehensively lost. We did, quite recently. And there was no one around, to ask directions, for over an hour except farmers far away across fields and a beagle standing guard in the middle of a silent village street. It is still no good going to Lot hoping for laid-on entertainment or many discos except in Cahors which, with a population of 21,000, is by far the biggest town. A particularly quiet area is Segala in the east – a region covered in huge chestnut trees, purple heather and thick broom with few people but some pleasant family-run hotels.

In Lot you will find peace, tranquillity, good regional cooking, good strong red wine of Cahors and air so pure that it, too, seems to intoxicate you. And you will find sunshine and warmth – Lot is further south than most people realise. Winters are relatively mild in the valleys, summers are hot and dry, spring and autumn are delightfully warm, and spring comes early. Lot to me is like a *Relais du Silence* – promising *Calme, Tranquilité, Repos*.

HOW TO GO

AIR

London–Bordeaux (Air France or British Airways) then train to Cahors via Montauban.
London–Toulouse (Air France, Dan Air) then train to Cahors or Brive.
Euroexpress (227 Shepherd's Bush Rd, London W6 7AS tel 01.748.2607) run charters to Bordeaux and Toulouse from Gatwick (London) May–October.

RAIL

TGV network of high-speed trains is to be extended shortly to Bordeaux and Montauban. At present Paris (Austerlitz)–Cahors takes 5hrs 10mins. Paris–Brive takes 4hrs–5½hrs.
French Motorail car-carrying trains run Boulogne–Brive in season.
Information French Railways, 179 Piccadilly, London W1V 0BA (tel. 01.409.5318).
Useful rail routes within Quercy are Cahors – Gourdon – Souillac; Brive – Rocamadour – Gramat – Figeac.

Road routes from the channel ports depend on personal choice and time available.

FOOD

Let's face it, Quercy and Périgord dishes are almost the same – but don't tell a Quercy or Périgord chef that! I did once, when I was younger and less diplomatic. I got a Quercynois five-course meal with a long lecture on the subtle differences of each dish from the *périgourdine* version from a superb chef in Cahors who, alas, has long since retired.

Both cuisines rely heavily on goose, duck and their fat, in which most dishes are cooked, and their livers. Both make *confits* of goose and duck – legs and wings preserved in their own fat, originally in stone jars, now in bottles or cans. And they force-feed geese and overfeed duck to produce *foie-gras* – the strong, rich liver which is a delight to gourmets and the horror of the English, who love the taste but are sickened by the feeding methods. They produce the best truffles in France and when they cannot afford to use this 'black diamond' they use strong fleshy *cèpes* or even lesser fungi-like *trompettes de la mort*, though this does nothing for the flavour of the dish. The subtlety of truffles is that they enhance the flavour of other ingredients.

Périgord and Quercy are both fond of stuffing poultry and meat and both produce succulent *terrines* and *charcuterie*.

The finest example in France of a poor peasant dish which has become a gourmet's delight is *Cou Farci* – stuffed goose neck, which can be served hot or, more usually, cold and sliced. In centuries past the peasant farmers could not afford to eat the geese which they produced. They saved for themselves only the

neck with its skin on and the giblets, which they chopped to stuff the neck, mixing them perhaps with bread, spirit made from local wine, a little pork if they were lucky enough to have any, garlic and a little chopped truffle, or *cèpes*, which must have been very much less valuable then. They tied up the end of the neck to make a sausage and fried it in a lot of goose fat for about one-and-a-half-hours. It could be kept preserved in the fat. And it was said in the countryside that if you had a goose neck, a loaf, of bread and a bottle of wine you could invite your neighbour to a feast. In the modern gourmet version from Quercy, you stuff the neck with about half a pound of minced pork and goose meat, nearly half a pound of *foie-gras*, an ounce of chopped truffles, an egg, some *marc* or brandy, and simmer it in goose fat for over an hour. At the current price of *foie-gras* and truffles, it is no longer a peasant dish!

Confit of goose or duck is delicious fried brown in its own fat and although they are not cheap, *confits* are well worth taking home in cans or glass jars. The fat left in the pan is used for frying slices of potatoes with garlic. Incidentally goose and duck fat can be bought by weight at the butchers or in tins at other shops. It gives a rich and special flavour to the simplest dishes. In Quercy they fry eggs in it with a little chopped onion, adding parsley and chopped garlic at the last moment. They are served with diced aubergines cooked in goose fat. In Lot-et-Garonne they call it *oeufs à l'agenaise*.

A delicious simple dish is *fricassés de cèpes à la Quercynoise* (*cèpes* browned in goose fat).

Confit of goose is made into *cassoulet* in Quercy, though it is not so famous as the *cassoulet* of Castelnaudry, Carcassonne or Toulouse. It contains white beans, of course, pork, bacon and sausage, and also mutton or lamb not included in the Toulouse version. A more usual bean dish and family standby is *sobronade*, a very thick soup of fresh and salt pork, vegetables (leeks, carrots, celery, turnips) and white beans, simmered indefinitely and served poured on to slices of bread. As in Périgord, soup is so popular that when people want to know if dinner is ready they say: 'Have you made the soup?'. A superb soup-stew is made from freshwater crayfish. An old peasant stew is *tourin* – onion and milk soup poured over slices of bread with grated cheese. The custom after soup is to *faire Chabrol* – pour wine in the soup bowl, swill it round and drink it.

Poule au pot, stuffed chicken poached with vegetables, which Henri IV wished every family in the land could have on Sunday, is as popular in Lot as in Périgord.

A superb dish is *pintade rôtie, flambée et bardée de truffes de Gourdon* – roast guinea hen stuffed with truffles of Gourdon (regarded as the best in Quercy), and served in flaming brandy sauce.

Goose, duck or chicken giblets and wings are cooked with potatoes, carrot and garlic to make *alicot* (or *alicuit*). Don't muddle it with *aligot* from the Rouergue and Auvergne (*aligot* cheese mixed with puréed potatoes and garlic). *Alicot* is even better, using turkey, which is becoming increasingly popular in Quercy, as in many parts of France.

Game tends to be 'farmed' these days – boar kept in pens, pheasant reared carefully, so it is easy to get *pâté de sanglier* (boar), *marcassin* (young boar) and *faisan* (pheasant). Tinned pâté is not necessarily from a factory. Restaurants do their own canning in season. So do shops (*boucheries* and *charcuteries*) and even some farmers' wives. Pâtés with *jus de truffes* does not have truffles in it but the liquid from canned truffles – often truffle-flavoured Madeira wine or brandy. Truffles do impart a flavour to the juice. Housewives making truffled omelettes wrap the eggs in their shells in a bag with truffles beforehand, swearing that the flavour gets through the shell. These omelettes should be cooked in goose fat (or at least pork fat) and the truffle chopped or sliced very thinly.

Beware of cheap 'truffled' pâtés. That other black fungus (*trompettes de la mort*) could have been substituted.

The great, old dish of Souillac is too expensive to be seen around much these days – *ragoût de truffes au Vieux Cahors*. It is made of large truffles simmered in the oven in a juice made of a bottle of old Cahors wine with chicken stock, lean gammon, garlic, thyme, parsley, finely chopped shallot, celery, leek, carrots and sliced small truffles. Superb! You drink old Cahors with it, of course.

Rillettes, most often made of pork, are often made in Quercy with shredded goose, pounded with goose fat and eaten on bread or toast – without butter.

Roquefort cheese comes from sheep's milk from all over France, but is matured in the Rouergue, outside Quercy. *Bleu de Quercy* (or *bleu de Causses*), made from cow's milk, is used as a Roquefort substitute in a very good cheese starter or savoury, served on toast, called *mousse aux noix*. The cheese is liquidised with butter, folded into whipped *crème fraîche* (slightly sour cream) and mixed with shelled walnuts.

Most desserts are of fruit, often bottled in *eau de vie*, but, as in Périgord, the simple fritters, *les merveilles*, are eaten hot or cold, especially on Shrove Tuesday (Mardi Gras).

You will certainly eat heartily in Quercy and there is certainly no lack of flavour. The dishes tend to be old-styled and straightforward.

CHEESES

Best-known cheeses next to *bleu de Quercy* are both called cabecou de Rocamadour, though made mostly in Gramat. In spring it is made from goats' milk, in summer from sheeps' milk, when it is nuttier and harder. Aged in *marc* in crocks, wrapped in leaves, it becomes *picadou*. It is very tasty – and smelly.

Bleu de Quercy – produced in Gourdon and Figeac commercially – soft, very savoury, blue, from cow's milk.

Cabecou de Livernon – goat cheese made by Quercy farmers. Similar to Rocamadour and very good.

Cabicou de Cahors (or *cabrichou*) – produced by farmers from goats' milk, full flavour, nutty, strongish smell.

Picadou de Quercy – made from either goats' or sheeps' milk. Sometimes aged in spirit wrapped in leaves, like Rocamadour cheese, which makes it very strong.

WINE

Cahors red wines have been loved by the English for centuries. Only very recently have they been 'discovered' by the French, partly because of a fashionable interest in 'country' wines and partly because a number of politicians and businessmen bought houses in Quercy as country hideouts.

The English, who occupied Quercy for so long, called it 'black wine' because of its deep purple colour when young.

The traditional old Cahors is aged in the wood, until the maker decides that it is ready for bottling, and this can alter with each vintage. True Vieux or Vieux Réserve has to mature for at least three years. The best should be kept in bottle at least another two years and is often at its best when ten years old.

This means a slow turnover of capital for winemakers, who are nearly always also the growers. It was not surprising then that with the fashion for light, young wines to go with *Nouvelle Cuisine*, some growers began to make Cahors wines lighter and to sell them young. They are called *Cahors Gouleyant* (almost untranslatable, meaning something like 'easy to drink, light and pleasant'). Personally, I thought that they were a failure. There

are more suitable red wines for drinking young, like the Chinons made from Gamay grapes. The best growers still make the glorious, subtly perfumed, refined wines and mature them. They make them mostly from Auxerrois grapes called Côt Noir or Malbec in other areas and once popular in Bordeaux. This gives a black, rather harsh wine, so it is tempered with Merlot, used so successfully in Bordeaux, especially St Emilion. This grape adds a softer, subtle touch and helps the wine to mature better and faster.

Along with the English, the Popes of Avignon and the Russians were also addicted. They still make Caorskoie in the Crimea where Lot vines were planted. Later the Bordeaux *négociants* bought Cahors wine to liven up pale, thin Bordeaux wines!

Last century the dreaded phylloxera disease devastated the vines, hitting Bordeaux and Bergerac too. Many hill vineyards were abandoned, and not until the 1950s did Cahors wines begin to recover. Improvement came fast after Cahors was classified as an *Appellation d'Origine Contrôlée* (AOC) wine in 1971.

Some families have been growing grapes for generations and produce not only great winemakers but great characters. The greatest is probably Jean Jouffreau, whose family have been *vignerons* at Prayssac for three hundred years. His Clos de Gamot vines were planted one hundred years ago. He uses no weedkillers and is the greatest expert at deciding how long the wine should age in the wood. The resulting wine is absolutely delightful – *gras*, as the French say – rich in alcohol and flavour, full-bodied and fleshy.

In 1971 the Jouffreau family bought the delightful Château de Cayrou (14th to 16th century) and its vineyard on gravelly soil from Comte André de Monpezat and it is now run by Jean Jouffreau's daughter and son-in-law. Excellent, modern equipment was installed and new underground cellars built. The result is great wine – especially 1979, the superb 1982 and 1985, which were still improving in 1989.

You can reach Château de Cayrou from Puy l'Évêque by driving down from the D911 through the village. Just before you reach the bridge over the Lot is a little road on the left, D28, marked to the château, which is also marked on yellow Michelin map 79. You can visit, taste wine and buy if you wish at any time in working hours. English is spoken (65.22.40.26). For Clos de Gamot, continue east from Puy l'Évêque on D911 for 5km to Prayssac, then take little D67 right to the river Lot. The Clos is also marked on yellow Michelin 79 and has the same tasting arrangement as Cayrou (65.22.40.26).

The Baldés family at Clos Triguedina have been in the business for eight generations, since 1830. They use a blend of modern and traditional methods, producing a perfectly balanced wine, superb with beef, duck or game. From forty-year-old vines they make a great special *cuvée* called Le Prince Probus.

One great character among *vignerons* is Georges Vigouroux, who is also a wine wholesaler, exporter and owner of the superb old Château de Mercuès, which he has made into a magnificent hotel, with splendid views over the Lot valley.

He bought a vineyard (Château La Haute Serre) at Cieurac, south of Cahors, in 1971 which had been abandoned for one hundred years. It was cleared of massive stones and rocks, tilled, planted and the grapes are handpicked. The result is a fruity but earthy wine which is pleasant drunk young but better when kept to become heavier, polished and strong.

His cellars are at Château Mercuès and you can taste and buy there – not only his own wine but others. Or you can visit his vineyards, taste and see a film on wines in English (twenty minutes). Take N20 south from Cahors to the airfield (12km). A signboard points along D149 left to Haute Serre.

Although Parisian interest in Cahors wines has put up their price, they are still excellent value.

A good place to taste a lot of them is the lovely country hotel La Pescalerie at Cabrerets (*see* page 69). The joint owner, Dr Roger Belcour, who runs a medical clinic in Cahors, is a true expert on Cahors wines, has an excellent cellar to accompany the beautiful meals at the hotel, and will advise you willingly.

Coteaux de Quercy are wines made around Cahors and to the south. The red is made with Gamay grape, so is light and fruity. So is the rosé.

Around Agen, in Lot-et-Garonne, Agenais Vins de Pays are

red (deep ruby and tannic) and dry white (pale, fruity, acidic and refreshing).

Coteaux de Quercy light red wine from below Cahors continues to be made southward in Tarn-et-Garonne from the Gamay grape used for Beaujolais and the lighter Chinon red wines in the Loire. The wines are light and fruity, with a nice colour, and make good value table wines. Rosé is made, too.

Around Montauban, red and rosé wines called Coteaux or Terrasses de Montauban are fruity and rather like Gaillac wines. From west of Montauban come the red, dry white and rosé wines of Saint-Sardon. The whites are rather similar to ordinary dry whites of Bordeaux.

All the wines are Vin de Pays. A little Côte de Frontonnais red, made mostly in Haute Garonne, is made also in Tarn-et-Garonne – fruity AOC red wines, quite cheap, can be drunk young but are better when three years old.

The best-known wine of Lot-et-Garonne is quite well known in Britain now. Côtes de Buzet red, dry white and rosé, are AOC wines which come from the area between Agen and Casteljaloux on the left bank of the Garonne. They have improved enormously, thanks to vinification by the Cave Co-operative at Buzet-sur-Baïse. The reds are made with the same grapes as red Bordeaux – Cabernet Sauvignon, Cabernet Franc and Merlot, with a very little Malbec. Buzets are underrated wines, with the elegance of Cabernet grapes and soft fruit of Merlot, and a splendid colour. They are excellent to drink with meat and turkey or chicken, best between three and eight years old. The vineyards are expanding because the wines are deservedly becoming more popular. They are excellent value. The special wine, Cuvée Napoléon, is aged in new oak casks like the best Bordeaux and is like a good Médoc.

You can taste Buzet at Les Vignerons des Côtes-de-Buzet (tel. 53.79.44.30) at Buzet-sur-Baïse, between A61 motorway and river Garonne on D962 on Baïse river (32km NW of Agen). The white is made from Sémillon, Sauvignon and Muscadelle grapes and is like ordinary white Bordeaux but a little heavier.

Duras wines are becoming well known in Britain, too – especially dry white wines. They only just sneak into Lot-et-Garonne, for Duras itself is right on the border of Gironde, the département which includes Bordeaux. The vineyards are between the vineyards of Entre-Deux-Mers (Bordeaux) and Bergerac. The red wines are made from the same grapes as Bordeaux and are like a simple Bordeaux – fruity, pleasant, easy to drink young. Twice as much white is produced. Years ago most of it was sweetish but with changing fashions the dry whites based on Sauvignon have taken over. To the Sauvignon are added Sémillon, Muscadelle and local grapes Mauzac, Ondenc and Ugni-Blanc (a grape giving crisp acidity and used for the wines distilled into Cognac). Duras wines are still not known extensively in France and are good value. They are worth seeking.

An underrated wine is Côtes du Marmandais from vines planted both side of the Garonne 35 to 40km upstream from Langon. It is VDQS wine (*Vin Délimité de Qualité Supérieure*), meaning wine from a defined area of named grapes and controlled quality, better than Vin de Pays, but not as good as Appéllation d'Origine Contrôlée (AOC). The red is made from a blend of up to eight grapes. It is pleasant with soft fruit and easy to drink. A very little cheap white is produced.

Wines labelled Agenais are Vins de Pays red, dry white or a very little rosé from around Agen and Villeneuve-sur-Lot.

PREHISTORY, HISTORY AND ART

The caves of Lot, like those of the Dordogne, were forgotten by man for centuries, but now that they have been explored again they have revealed many secrets of our prehistoric ancestors of 40,000 to 150,000 years ago.

Les Eyzies in the Dordogne is rightly called 'The Capital of Prehistory' for the wealth of evidence of early man's way of living that its caves have revealed. There were discovered the tools men fashioned in bone and chipped stone, jewellery and the evidence of animals he hunted (elephants, mammoth, horses, bisons, oxen, rhinoceros, bear, deer and reindeer). Human and animal skeletons were found, and remarkable wall engravings, sculptures and paintings, mostly of animals, some of great realism and even beauty.

Cave paintings

There is nothing so revealing in Lot. But there is the great Padirac cave with its underground river, a refuge for people from marauding soldiers and robbers in many wars. Lacave caves have tools and weapons showing that man lived here 40,000 years ago; Pech-Merle cave where prehistoric man is believed to have performed religious rites; Presque cave near St Céré, with its remarkable stalactites and stalagmites, and Cougnac caves only 3km from Gourdon, where prehistoric men drew deer, elephants and people in ochre and black.

In the Dark Ages and Middle Ages these caves were used as shelters during various tribal invasions, and again when the rival Capet and Plantagenet families were fighting for power in France and fighting between themselves for power in France and England.

Families took refuge in them, particularly in the Hundred Years War which broke out in 1337 when Edward III of England claimed the French throne through inheritance from his French mother, and which continued until 1453 when Joan of Arc and then the French troops of her 'Dauphin', Charles VII, finally drove the English out. The villagers hid not only from the pillaging English troops but also from the French and especially the troops of the mercenary barons who raised armies called *Les*

Routiers which fought and pillaged wherever they could find the most loot. Many caves were used later in the Religious Wars, when most of the ordinary people of Quercy were on the Protestant side.

Then for centuries the caves were unused, perhaps forgotten. Frightening legends grew up about them and peasants were afraid to enter them.

Back in 51 BC Julius Caesar's Roman Armies took Quercy in their conquest of Gaul and the Pax Romana lasted six centuries. Luzech, Vayrac and Capdenac were three towns which started as Roman forts. Cahors was an important, flourishing Gallo-Roman town. It was called Divona Caducorum (Sacred Spring) and Gauls and Romans worshipped at the source, which still supplies Cahors with drinking water. Later the town was called simply Cadurca, which became Cahors.

When the Roman Empire collapsed, Quercy suffered five centuries of invasion by Visigoths, Franks, Arabs and Norsemen. Feudal barons took it over and it became a fairly flourishing area in the 12th and 13th centuries. But in the Hundred Years War it was a battleground. The English held much of it and a number of places are still called 'Château des Anglais'. Apart from pillage, famine, disease and cholera hit towns and villages, and the Black Death spreading across Europe to France and England actually stopped the war for a few years. At the end of the war, Quercy was decimated. Three-quarters of its churches were abandoned. Only six people remained in the town of Gramat. 'Immigrants' were brought in from the Auvergne, Rouergue and Languedoc.

Although Quercy was feudal, the local lords were not very important and their peasants were very free by most standards. The economy prospered and with it came an artistic and literary renaissance. Cahors University was famous and flourishing by the 16th century. Beautiful houses from that period of Renaissance still stand in Cahors, St Céré and Figeac. The beautiful Château of Montal was built in 1323–34 (*see* page 29). Then in 1560, little more than a hundred years after the end of the Hundred Years War came the Religious Wars between the Catholics and the Calvinist Protestants. Both Périgord and Quercy (Dordogne and Lot) were mostly Protestant. Atrocities were committed on both sides and many beautiful buildings were destroyed. Calvinists destroyed treasures in churches believing them to be 'ungodly'. Henri de Navarre, the great Protestant General, had a number of castles razed so that the Catholics could not use them. The extremists of the Catholic League formed by the Duc de Guise were particularly vicious and feared, and in the end were fighting against the Royal Catholic troops of Henri III of France. There was fighting in Cahors, Figeac, Gramat, Castelnau, Capdenac, Martel.

The Bishop of Cahors, Antoine Hébrard de St Sulpice, member of a famous, powerful family who still own the mediaeval castle at St Sulpice in the Célé valley in the Lot, did manage to negotiate a truce between the Royal troops and the Leaguers. But Henri de Navarre ended the Wars by becoming a Catholic to gain the crown as Henri IV. He kept the loyalty of his Protestant followers, and by the Edict of Nantes made Protestantism legal in France. In Quercy he gave the Calvinists four *places de sûreté* – secure retreats where they could practise their faith unhindered. They were Montauban (now in Tarn-et-Garonne), Figeac, Cajarc and Cardaillac. But the Quercynois hated the central rule of Paris and when Henri IV died they revolted for independence, not for religious beliefs. Louis XIII besieged Montauban unsuccessfully but in 1629 the revolt was crushed by Richelieu. Local traditions were quashed, too.

The people of Quercy, like those of Perigord, were desperately poor. Peasants were near to starvation because of huge rents demanded by landowners and the corrupt tax-collecting system which made the tax collectors rich while the Royal coffers were emptied by wars. Twice the peasants revolted without success (1594 and 1636).

The landowners took two-thirds of what the peasants produced on their land. Even farmers' families lived on *miques*, dumplings made of chestnut or maize flour mixed with a little fat and boiled. Every crop failure meant starvation. Even skilled craftsmen were destitute and took to hills and forests as goatherds or charcoal burners. In 1685 when the Edict of Nantes was revoked and Protestantism was illegal again, most of the skilled workers, who were Protestants, fled to Holland or England, leaving no one to produce the wealth for many communities.

The Revolution was welcomed. The peasants attacked the castles, looted the houses of the landowners and governing classes who had extracted outrageous rents from them, and attacked the rich abbeys and big churches. Village clergy and churches were left alone, for the clergy, too, were poor and oppressed. But the Revolution did not make the people of Quercy any richer.

Last century small iron and steel industries grew up where there were oaks to be cut, but then coal replaced charcoal, the industry moved to the industrial north near the coalfields and young workers from Quercy followed. In the 1850s phylloxera, the aphid which destroys vines, spread from the Midi and Bordeaux, destroying two-thirds of Lot vineyards. Many of them have never produced grapes again.

During the Second World War Dordogne and Quercy became very important Resistance areas, their caves used for hiding men and arms. The RAF used particularly the Padirac and St Céré areas for dropping supplies. On 14th July 1944, one hundred tons of arms were dropped at Padirac alone. The Hôtel de Paris at St Céré (now Coq Arlequin et Paris and still run by the great hoteliers and chefs, the Bizat family) was a secret headquarters of Colonel Buckmaster's British Supply and Intelligence Organisation for the Resistance.

After the war, good money in booming factories of the north lured away the young, who could see little future in working uneconomic farm units so shrunk by inheritance. Much of the marginal land was abandoned. The wine business is doing better now but Quercy relies quite a lot on summer tourists and people with second homes, though not so heavily as the Dordogne does. So it remains a quiet, peaceful, attractive land, underpopulated, which adds to its charm.

Lot has not produced many famous artists or writers. But the great classical painter Ingres was born in 1780 in Montauban, as was the sculptor and painter Émile Bourdelle (1861–1929). François Maynard (1582–1646), conventional love poet, lived in St Céré for some years. Clément Marot the poet was born in Cahors in 1497. His witty satires made him many enemies and his translation of the psalms into French got him into trouble with the Church.

More recently, the great painter Jean Lurçat, who revived so brilliantly the old art of tapestry, set up his studio and workshop in St Laurent tower high on a hill above St Céré and you can see many of his works there and in the Casino bar-gallery. He died in St Céré in 1966.

Detail from Jean Lurçat's Spirit of France

Cahors

[MAP 2, page 146]

To see Cahors in its superb setting, its towers and belfries, old houses and bridges almost encircled by a great loop of the river Lot, you must climb the hills above it.

There are two superb viewing spots. The first is to the north. Just beyond the old fortifications Barbacane and Tour St Jean in Cahors, take N20 Brive road for just 100 metres, then fork right on the little V10 local road. Quite soon you get superb views over the valley and town. Continue and you have views over surrounding hills and the Lot valley.

Another good view can be seen from Mont St Cyr, where there is a viewing table. Cross the south bridge Pont Louis Philippe, turn left on D6, then left again after 1.5km. Keep going left for another 2km. You can see how the town is divided into old and new quarters, and in the background you can see the magnificent Valentré bridge, the most beautiful fortified medieval bridge in France. To see the bridge better, turn left for a little way along the river bank before crossing it from inside the river loop. There is another superb bridge and river view if you cross the Valentré bridge and turn right for about 150 metres along the river bank on D8.

Valentré was started in 1308 and is another of many bridges which that busy engineer Satan helped to build. After fifty years the bridge was not completed and the architect was in despair. Like so many others he made a pact with Satan, who promised to bring all the materials the architect ordered to the site in return for the architect's soul. The Devil should have known better than to trust the man. When the bridge was just about finished he ordered Satan to bring him water in a sieve. The Devil tried

Valentré Bridge, Cahors

twice but failed. So he gave up after knocking the top stone off the centre tower. Each time the stone was replaced it fell off again until the bridge was restored. Then the stone on the Devil's tower was firmly fixed and a little figure of a devil trying to dislodge it carved on the corner. Perhaps the Devil had the last laugh, for in 1360 within two years of completion, the bridge and town were handed to the English under the Treaty of Brétigny.

Valentré was built as a fort to defend the town as much as a river crossing and it was never captured. Originally there was a barbican on the town side but that was replaced by a gate when the bridge was modified to take more traffic in 1879. It has three square towers with four-sided pointed caps. Each one was originally closed by gates and portcullises and the central tower was a look-out post. It was protected on the left bank by out-works and a guard house.

Cahors had a lot to protect in those days. In the 13th century Lombard bankers and merchants had moved in and made it the most important banking centre in Europe. The bankers lent money to the Pope and to kings and Cahors banks had branches ('counting houses') all over Europe. Even the Black Death, which killed many citizens, did not destroy its golden age. In 1332 the university was founded by Jacques Duèze, native of Cahors, who had become Pope John XXII – an Avignon Pope. But under the Treaty of Brétigny all Quercy came under English rule. The King of France had to order the consuls of Cahors to hand over the keys of the town. They protested: 'We are not abandoning the King. He is abandoning us to a foreign master'.

A lot of the people left. When the English left Quercy in 1450 Cahors was almost ruined. But the English did take with them a strong liking for Cahors wine and continued to be Cahors' greatest customer until the wine became fashionable in Paris two or three years ago. Wine is still Cahors' major business.

In 1580 Huguenots sacked Cahors. The city's decline had begun in earnest.

The city has grown livelier lately, with more traffic, but it remains basically a happy provincial town where you sit in the sun under the plane trees outside a café on boulevard Gambetta, the main street, and do not worry too much about time. Gambetta is the street which divides old Cahors from the newer area, and it was named after Cahors' most famous son.

Léon Michel Gambetta, born in Cahors in 1838 of a Genoese-Jewish family, must have as many streets or squares in France named after him as Victor Hugo and Général de Gaulle. Like de Gaulle, he was a national hero and freedom fighter who fell from power finally by trying to change the French Constitution.

As a young man, he became so fascinated when he visited a courtroom that he decided to become a lawyer. He practised at the Paris bar, where he was known for advanced liberal views, and had great courtroom success defending opponents of Napoleon III's regime. He was elected a deputy. When Napoleon III surrendered to the Prussians he was one of the proclaimers of the Republic on 4 September 1870, and became Minister of the Interior in the Government of National Defence. And when the Prussians were besieging Paris and people were near to starvation he escaped by balloon to Tours to continue the fight. He had some victories but his amateur army was crushed by the powerful Prussians, so he went to Bordeaux and proclaimed a Republican Government with a decree disenfranchising all royal dynasties. His Paris colleagues repudiated it and he fled to Spain in 1871. But he was re-elected by no fewer than ten separate départements of France. He became leader of the Republican Union and formulated a Republican policy regarded in those days as outrageously advanced. It included separation of the church and state, liberty of meeting and of the press, removal of laws banning trade unions and compulsory free education. His party was the biggest in the Chamber, with 220 members, but the Republican president François Grèvy who was much less radical, disliked his policies and disliked him, so kept him out of office. He had previously insulted the reactionary president, the old soldier Marshal MacMahon who wanted to bring back the monarchy, and was sent to prison for it. Immediately he was released the people re-elected him to the Chamber. He was, it seems, volatile and even some of his fellow Republicans called him 'raving mad' ('*fou furieux*').

At last in 1881 he became prime minister, but he could not get Republicans with the right talent to serve with him. He started by trying to alter the method of election of deputies. France in those days had the present British system of first-past-the-post in single constituencies. He wanted fairer elections by proportional representation and regional lists of candidates.

The deputies' own seats were in danger. They threw out the bill and he resigned. He died the same year, 1882, from a septic wound. He was forty-four.

The old town to the east of boulevard Gambetta still looks medieval. The Cathedral of St Stephen, started at the end of the 11th century, has a severe Gothic façade because it was intended by Bishop Gérard of Cardaillac to be a fortress to shelter people in times of trouble. The Byzantine domed roof helps to save it from looking too fort-like. So does the marvellous north doorway, often compared to the portal of the abbey church at Moissac in Tarn-et-Garonne. It is divided into panels. The centre panel shows the Ascension of Christ with angels each side and the Virgin and apostles below in arcades. Small cherubs are coming from the clouds to welcome Christ. Scenes all round show the life and martyrdom of St Étienne (St Stephen).

Inside, the nave is topped with two domes while the choir is decorated with paintings and lit by stained glass windows. The frescoes in the west dome showing the stoning to death of St Étienne and eight huge figurines of prophets were uncovered in 1872 after being hidden for years by coats of whitewash.

The fine Flamboyant cloisters were damaged by the Huguenots but recently restored.

The other main church, St Barthélemy in the upper town, is mostly 16th century. It has a fine brick belfry and there are good views over the Lot valley and the suburb of Cabessut over the river. Next to the church is the thirty-four metre high Tour de Jean XXII, all that remains of this Pope's family mansion. This Jean XXII was an unsavoury Pope, though he did introduce Cahors wine for Papal communions. Alleging sorcery, he had the Bishop of Cahors flayed and torn apart by wild horses.

Maison de Roaldès, owned in the 17th century by the well-known Quercy family of Roaldès, was built in the 15th century and restored in 1912. It has two interesting façades, one with timber framing and a balcony topped by a large round tower, the other with mullioned windows and doors and a rose window. This is in a pretty part of Cahors.

Les Badernes, the south-east area of the loop, was the commercial centre in the golden age and is being restored.

In the 14th century the open side of the town not guarded by the river Lot was fortified. The Barbacane, an elegant guard-house, and Tour St-Jean, built on a rock overlooking the river, remain. They are by the N20 as you enter the town. Just off N20, 10km north of the town at St-Pierre-Lafeuille, are the massive round towers of the medieval Château de Roussillon, restored by the Gontaut-Biron family.

Market days are lively in Cahors. They are held on the Cathedral square.

TOURIST INFORMATION 1 pl. Aristide-Briand (65.35.09.56)
MARKETS Wednesday, Saturday. Truffle and Foie-Gras Markets (November–end February) Saturday
FESTIVALS Mid-July – Blues Festival. June–August – Painting Exhibitions in Grenier du Chapitre

HOTEL

Terminus, Restaurant Balandre, 5 ave Charles-de-Freycinet (Hotel 65.35.24.50; restaurant 65.30.01.97). Charming *fin-de-siècle* hotel, rooms modernised with taste. To lighten Quercy dishes and add modern touches is a difficult trick which young Gilles Marre performs in Le Balandre. ROOMS B–E. MEALS C–F. Restaurant shut Sunday evenings, Monday off-season; Saturday lunch in summer; 20–30 June; 1–20 February.

RESTAURANT

La Taverne, 1 rue Jean-Baptiste-Delpech (65.35.28.66). Neither Michelin nor Gault-Millau now mention the one-time temple of the great Escorbiac. But my favourite French critic Marc Champérard likes it and so do I. All the treasures of Quercy (truffles, *foie-gras*, *confits*, *cèpes*, *cassoulets*) plus dishes according to the market. Sensible prices. Superb Cahors wines. MEALS C–G. Shut Sunday evening low season.

St Céré

[MAP 2, page 146]

St Céré is a delight – a smiling little town with the river Bave running through its streets, flower-decked riverside houses and a big, lively square where a Saturday market which spreads to the whole town centre brings in sellers, buyers, friends and gossips from the whole neighbouring countryside. It's a wonderful place to stay and to explore the Lot countryside and quiet stretches of the Dordogne river. I could imagine myself retiring here to settle down and write.

It has lovely houses from the 15th to 17th centuries, some

with wooden-corbelled façades and topped with roofs of small brown tiles, in charming little squares or with the river washing their walls. The turreted 15th-century Puymule mansion in place de l'Église, the Ambert mansion with two corbelled turrets and a Renaissance doorway in rue de Mazel are particularly attractive. Impasse Langarouste, a cul-de-sac off rue Mazel with a stream running through it is lined with tall corbelled houses.

Rue St Cyr is lined with old houses, too, including the 15th-century Miramon mansion with a corner turret. Place du Mercadial at the end of St Cyr and rue de Mazel was where fishermen sold their catch from a stone slab along the 15th-century house of Jean de Séguier (a rich merchant) on the corner of rue Pasteur. The Bave river must have had more and bigger fish in those days, though the Dordogne itself and its tributary the Cère are only 8km north. From this corner you can see St Laurent Towers, to which St Céré owes much of its safety over centuries. Even in the Hundred Years War it was not badly damaged.

The town was founded in the 9th century and in the 13th century the very powerful Viscounts of Turenne gave it the franchise and many privileges, including the right to set up trading houses and hold lucrative fairs. Local consuls ran the town. St Laurent Towers were built standing high on a hill, with strong ramparts below. St Laurent was called Château de St Séré, with an 'S'. The town was then called Ste Spérie, after the daughter of a local lord of the 8th century. The English occupied it from 1369–1378 and in the Wars of Religion in 1575 the Protestants took over château and town and destroyed the relics of Ste Spérie. Then the château was almost destroyed when the Catholic League commander Duc de Mayenne took it back in 1586. The two towers remaining became 'Tours St Laurent' and the town 'St Séré'. But it seems that a clerk copying the official records wrote 'St Céré' for the town and 'St Cère' for the 'St Sère' river and they have been spelt that way since! After the Revolution, Paris said that a saint's name was 'fanatical' and changed the name to 'Franc-Céré' but the town took no notice.

In 1945 the towers of St Laurent became the home and studio of Jean Lurçat, the painter and tapestry and ceramic artist who died there in 1966. Here he designed his magnifgicent, richly coloured tapestries which revived and revolutionised the old art, including his very controversial series of tapestries called 'Song of the World', showing a modern view of the world and how it will end. He designed these after he had seen the medieval tapestry series 'The Apocalypse' in Angers on the Loire. His own series is now shown in that city and are the centre of much debate, probably more political than artistic. Lurçat was left wing. His tapestries are superb.

There is a Jean Lurçat museum in Angers, a Jean Lurçat Cultural Centre and a tapestry museum in the traditional tapestry-weaving town of Aubusson in the Upper Creuze Valley. Now there is a museum of Lurçat's tapestries and ceramics, with a short film, in Tours St Laurent. Down in the town, in the bar-gallery of the Casino, is another Lurçat exhibition. Here you can walk round and admire his work with a glass in your hand, without going near the gaming tables, which are over the road. And you can see two of his best works and some cartoons in the Hôtel de Paris et du Coq Arlequin. They include the Coq himself, puffed up in a coat of many colours. The Bizat family have owned the hotel for well over one hundred years. Gérard, the father, was himself a professional artist and a great friend of Lurçat. His son Eric now does the cooking in this splendid hotel which was a secret British and Resistance headquarters in World War Two (*see* page 19). Gérard also sells his confit of duck and goose, foie-gras and various truffled and non-truffled terrines and pâtés, all from his own kitchens, in a little shop beside the hotel. And a welcome addition for St Céré's visitors and townsfolk is his new Grill du Coq Arlequin near the Château de Montal – an elegant country park with a large swimming pool, tennis, snack bar, bar and restaurant.

The church of Ste Spérie founded in the 12th century, is still in the town but was much rebuilt in Gothic style in 17th to 18th centuries. Buried beneath the chancel is the poet François Maynard. One of the earliest Academicians, Maynard spent many years in St Céré, dying there in 1646. He became secretary to Marguerite de Valois, first wife of Henri de Navarre (later Henri IV) and a court poet, nominated by Richelieu for the new Academy which the Cardinal had founded. These poets and writers were expected to write as Richelieu told them. They were in a sense his publicity men. But it seems that Maynard fell out with him – not for this reason but because he thought that Richelieu was not giving him enough gifts or honours. Maynard left Paris for St Céré and became a lion of literary circles, invited to the receptions at Château de Castelnau which rivalled even those on the Loire.

A beautiful château where there were fewer reasons for celebration was Château de Montal, a superb Renaissance manor 3km west of St Céré.

Jeanne de Balsac d'Entraygues brought up five children in a feudal stronghold here after being widowed in 1510. While her eldest son Robert was away fighting with François I in Italy, she had Montal rebuilt for him, bringing in architects, artists and builders from the great châteaux of the Loire. By 1534 her masterpiece was ready and she watched from a high window for his return.

The French were defeated at the Battle of Pavia. François was taken prisoner. Robert de Balsac d'Entraygues was killed. Only his body returned to Montal. His mother had the window

Château de Montal

blocked up and beneath it were carved the words 'Hope No More'. Her second son, Dordé, was in the church. The Pope absolved him from his vows so that he could continue the great family line. But the family sold Montal in 1593.

Many well-known Quercy families owned it, but it became uninhabitable after looting and depredation in the Revolution and in 1879 was sold to a Paris asset-stripper called Macaire who sold its treasures and even its stones for other buildings.

In 1908 Maurice Fenaille, a petrol millionaire, bought what remained. He then set about finding and buying back at ransom prices all the treasures and artistic pieces from collections and museums all round the world and had the château rebuilt as it was. One stone dooorway was missing. So he asked Rodin, the great sculptor, to make another. When it was ready in 1913, he gave it to the nation.

The château has two wings linked at the corner by a square tower containing a magnificent decorated Renaissance staircase in light Carennac stone. The stone roofs are steep. Above them are massive towers with loopholes. The richly decorated façade is glorious, the inner courtyard a Renaissance delight. The frieze above the ground floor is 32 metres long with a variety of carvings from a capital to a human head. The mullion windows of the first floor have bays between them containing family busts of Jeanne herself, her husband, her sons and her parents. Inside are Renaissance and Louis XIII furniture, paintings and plates by Bernard Palissy, the Huguenot pioneer of art in enamel, and excellent Tours and Flemish tapestries (open 1 March–31 October. Shut Saturday except in July, August).

La Grotte de Presque, 5km from St Céré along the attractive D673 road to Rocamadour, is not the most spectacular cave in the area but very pleasant to visit because it's more easily accessible than some others, with no slippery paths or steps.

Its chambers and galleries which go back 350 metres into the rocks have imaginative names like Salle des Draperies (Drapery Chamber), La Salle Haute (High Chamber), Salle de la Grand Cuve (Chamber of the Great Basin), Salle de Marbre Rouge (Red Marble Hall) and Salle des Merveilles (Hall of Wonder). They are justified, for the stalagmite columns seem carved in curious and beautiful shapes and even the walls seem to be decorated. At the entrance to the Hall of Wonder are indeed wonderful slender columns of dazzling whiteness. Rediscovered in 1825, it is the most charming of the Lot and Dordogne caves. Pierre Benoit described it as the Palace of Athenae (closed from 1st Sunday in October–Palm Sunday).

TOURIST INFORMATION place de la République (65.38.11.85) – shut mornings low season
MARKET Saturday
FESTIVALS August – Music Festival

HOTELS

Coq Arlequin, 1 boulevard du Dr Roux (65.38.02.13). Superb Quercy dishes; pleasant atmosphere. Excellent Cahors wines. ROOMS C–F. MEALS C–F. Shut January, February, Monday in winter.

Figeac

[MAP 2, page 147]

Little Figeac, which grew around a monastery in the 9th century, rises in terraces above the Célé river. The only town of any size on the river and still growing. But, alas, its modern suburbs are not worthy of the old town which they surround.

Its position, almost on the borders of Haut-Quercy and the Auvergne, with the Lot river only 7km south, has made it a popular business and tourist centre but there are still only 11,000 people living there. Canoeing and fishing, as well as river scenery, lure the tourists, for the Célé is an attractive river in a delightful valley, with old villages perched on cliffs and old mills by the water.

The town was ruled by the abbey until 1301 when Philippe IV of France took it over, and it has a tradition of fighting for freedom. Bands of English soldiers occupied it in the Hundred Years War. Then in the Wars of Religion it was Protestant and suffered much damage which was repaired later. Henri IV made it one of the '*places de sûreté*' reserved for Protestants. The people's resistance to the Germans in World War II earned the town the Croix de Guerre, but the Nazis deported six hundred townspeople to German slave-labour camps in 1944.

The huge 11th-century abbey church of St Sauveur suffered much in the Wars of Religion but the 17th and 19th century restorations do not really stand out from the surviving 12th to 14th century parts, and the Romanesque and Gothic blend to make the church very pleasant.

In place Vival, just back from the Célé's right bank, is the most interesting building, Hôtel de la Monnaie, a mint dating from the Royal takeover in 1301. Here money was minted for both French and English kings. Conveniently, the tourist office is now here and so is a small museum with pieces of sculpture from old church buildings and houses.

Many of the little old streets up the hill from Hôtel de la Monnaie and St Sauveur church to the old church of Notre-Dame du Puy are lined with charming half-timbered houses with balconies. Look especially for Hôtel Dumont de Sournac (14th century – No. 4 rue Clermont), houses in rue Gambetta, Hôtel du Viguier du Roi (14th century – No. 3 rue Delzhens), houses in rue Séguier and, in place Carnot, the towered 17th-century Maison Cisteron which belonged to a Protestant who was protected by Louis XIV because of his ability as a gunsmith and armourer. For anyone like me with an interest in old houses and a love of rivers Figeac and its surroundings are worth wandering around for several days. You had to be careful before 1945, for some of the narrow alleys such as Trou de la Belle were haunts of vagrants and thieves. Rue Emile-Zola now has artisan shops as in medieval times.

In place Champollion where rue Gambetta and rue Emile-Zola meet is a Commanderie of the Knights Templars Order with beautiful windows and, in a cul-de-sac, the house where the Champollion brothers, the great Egyptologists, were born. It is now a museum containing the exhibits which were until recently in Hôtel de la Monnaie.

Jean-François Champollion, born in Figeac in 1790, was a remarkable man who, alas, died at the age of forty-two. When he was fourteen he already had a command of Greek, Latin, Hebrew, Arabic, Chaldean and Syrian. At nineteen he was Professor of History at Grenoble University but was expelled in 1816 for Napoleonic sympathies. He had written two books on Egypt. He and the English physicist Thomas Young undertook the deciphering of a basalt tablet found near Rosetta in the Nile valley, which bore three inscriptions in ancient Egyptian hieroglyphics, Greek and cursive script. He discovered that the texts were identical. The Rosetta stone is in the British museum. A copy is in this house. He went to Egypt and deciphered many more texts. When he died his brother Jean-Jacques Champollion-Figeac continued his work on Egypt. He was librarian at the Palace of Fontainebleau.

Two 12th-century obelisks nearly 15 metres tall still remain from the days of the Benedictine monastery. They marked the boundaries of the monastery land and beyond them nobody could pursue an enemy. You can see one of them from D922 which runs to the Lot river south of Figeac. It is called Aiguille (needle) de la Côte de Cingle (or du Pressoir).

Westward along D13 is a 15th to 16th century castle, Ceint d'Eau, rising above the Célé valley.

Figeac was known before 1940 almost solely as the birthplace of the film actor Charles Boyer, the screen personification of the great French lover.

TOURIST INFORMATION Hôtel de la Monnaie, place Vival (65.34.06.25). Shut mornings out of season

HOTEL

Carmes, Enclos des Carmes (65.34.20.78). Outstanding cooking in modern hotel. Individual touches added to great Quercy dishes. Superb Cahors wines. MEALS C–F. ROOMS E. Shut Sunday evening, Saturday in winter; 15 December–15 January.

RESTAURANT

L'Escapade, route de Cahors (65.34.23.42). Rustic restaurant with gorgeous terrace. Classic old-style cooking at old-style prices. MEALS A–D. Shut Monday.

Souillac

[MAP 2, page 146]

Astride the N20 on the banks of the Dordogne river, with farming hamlets all round for miles, Souillac is inevitably a busy market and shopping centre for farming families and, in season, for tourists who flock in for miles from gîtes and camp sites. The queues for the banks can be awesome. So can the traffic for such a small town. But it is a happy, jostling place, the shops are family-run, and the market is the main one for a very wide and fertile area.

It got its name from a local word *souilh*, meaning a mire where wild boar wallow, and grew up around a Benedictine Abbey plundered and looted often by the English in the Hundred Years War. But Souillac became prosperous as a river trading centre. From the Auvergne, timber barrel staves and wine stakes were brought downriver and unloaded at Souillac. Here they were transferred to bigger *gabares*, flat-bottomed boats propelled by a pole, to be transported downstream to Bergerac, Libourne and Bordeaux, along with wine, corn, sheep and cattle. Some boats had single sails and carried passengers. Most Dordogne *gabares* were broken up at the end of their journey for their timber. The boatman would buy a mule and return on it, selling it to a farmer. The Souillac *gabares* were stronger and brought back salt, an expensive item inland in those days.

The journey of 200km from Souillac to Libourne usually took three days and was dangerous. I helped to take a modern *gabare* down the Dordogne a few years ago. It was of light, strong alloy and had a small auxiliary engine but I still spent much of my time waist or chest deep in icy waters *en tremblant*, which meant poling, shaking and coaxing the craft off shingle banks where currents had taken us.

There were many danger spots of choppy, fast-moving waters for the Souillac boatmen. The worst was downstream of Mauzac where there is 100 metres of rapids (Saut de Gratusse). Many lives were lost until the Lalinde canal was built in the 1840s to avoid the stretch.

Coming back was the real test for the Souillac men. *Bouviers-Haleurs* (local farmers) provided teams of oxen to tow the boat, each towing for about 3 to 6km. To avoid cliffs, the towpath moved from one side to another, so the boats had to cross – a very tricky operation achieved with a long pole.

The return journey to Souillac took three weeks and there was only a stretch of a month or so in the year when it could be done, for in winter floods and fast waters made it impossible and in summer there was too little water. The boatmen of Souillac earned their profits the hard way. The coming of the railway from Bordeaux to Brive further north killed the trade.

Souillac Abbey was burned down in the Wars of Religion in 1572. Only the church survived. It was rebuilt in the 17th century but closed in the Revolution. The church is now used as the Parish church. Of the former Parish church destroyed in the Wars of Religion, only the belfry exists. The old abbey church, now called Sainte-Marie, is very impressive – one of the finest churches in Lot or Dordogne. Mostly 12th-century it is Romanesque-Byzantine, rather like the much 'restored' Périgueux cathedral and Cahors. Its main strong, squat tower is surmounted by three deep domes. The effect is very Eastern-Orthodox. The grey stone can look severe in winter, silvery in summer sun.

L'Abbatiale Ste-Marie, Souillac

Inside, the nave has three magnificent domes which give it a lovely airy look, though it is not of the immense size of the cathedral in Cahors. It is fairly simply decorated, apart from the inner door. Between statues of St Peter and St Benedict this door has a bas-relief telling the story of the Monk Theophilus, Deacon of Adana monastery in Cilicia. Because of rumours that he was fiddling the books, this monk was removed from his job as treasurer of the monastery. He was so angry that he signed a pact with the Devil to get his job back. Then he repented and prayed to the Virgin Mary, who appeared to him in his sleep with St Michael and two guardian angels who brought his pact with the signature wiped out. She told him that he was pardoned.

One of the pillars of the doors has some mysterious and ferocious animal monsters chewing each other up.

Château de la Treyne, 6km from Souillac along D43, is a delightful little medieval-looking château perched on a cliff running straight down to the Dordogne river. And it has been made into a lovely hotel. It stands in a pretty park and looks especially beautiful from the river bridge. Although it was started in the 14th century, much of it was built in the 17th.

Another 5km east along D43 is Belcastel, another proud castle on top of a vertical cliff above the Dordogne where the river Ouysse joins it. Much of the château was rebuilt last century but part of the main wing and the chapel are from the Middle Ages. The château is in a beautiful setting with its white cliffs reflected in the silver river below. From its terrace, which you can visit, you have magnificent views of the two rivers and the surrounding hills and valleys. You can visit the chapel, too. A stone's throw from the castle, where the Dordogne river makes a deep cut through the Gramat Causse, are the caves called Grottes de Lacave.

A student of the great cave explorer E. A. Martel rediscovered them in 1902 and later prehistoric tools and weapons were found in them. They were from the Upper Palaeolithic Period of around 40,000 years ago.

A small railway and lift take you to an underground platform from which you can explore galleries a mile long on foot. You can imagine that the strangely shaped rocks are people, animals, buildings and villages. One group of chambers has stalagmites and stalactites, the other has underground rivers and pools. Salle du Lac is deeply impressive. Around a lake fluorescent rocks glow in the dark. In Salle des Merveilles (Hall of Wonders) are some beautiful and unusual shapes. Altogether there are twelve halls of 2000 square metres with dimmed lights and the colours and reflections are so enchanting that they have been called the Halls of Fairyland. They are not as cold as some caves – about 55 degrees F (13°C), so are pleasant to walk round (open 1 April–mid-October; visits take an hour).

TOURIST INFORMATION Souillac – 9 boulevard Malvy (65.37.81.56).
MARKET Monday, Wednesday, Friday
FESTIVALS July – Jazz Festival. June–August – Paintings *salon* in Town Hall

HOTELS

Les Granges Vieilles, route de Sarlat, 1.5km W on D703 (65.37.80.92). Peace in a large park with tall trees. ROOMS C–F. MEALS B–F. Shut 2–31 January.

Vieille Auberge, pl.Minoterie (65.32.79.43). Adapted Quercy regional cooking. ROOMS C–D. MEALS C–E. Shut 1 January–15 March; Sunday dinner, Monday in winter.

Auberge du Puits, 5 pl.Puits (65.37.80.32). Cheap, good-value regional meals; inn. ROOMS B–C. MEALS A–E. Shut Sunday evening, Monday low season; November, December.

At Lacave

Château de la Treyne on D43 (65.32.66.66). *See* page 19. Charming. Dine by candlelight. Swimming pool. Very expensive. ROOMS G. MEALS E–G. Shut mid-November–end March.

Pont de l'Ouysse, Lacave (65.37.87.04). Superb cooking with superb Quercy ingredients. Summer meals on terrace above the river. Sensible prices. Bedrooms modernised. Nice atmosphere. ROOMS E–G. MEALS C–F. Shut Monday off-season; mid-November–1 March.

Agen

[MAP 3, page 148]

Agen, a busy market town, has always been an important transport junction, halfway between Toulouse and Bordeaux, and now the A62 motorway passes alongside. Its railway line is still important and the Garonne lateral canal runs through it, crossing the Garonne river on an impressive aqueduct, 500 metres long with twenty-three arches. It is also still the market town for the early fruit and vegetables grown in the *pays des Serres*, bordered by the valleys of the Lot and Garonne. The fruit is superb – especially peaches, white table grapes called Chasselas, and plums, from which are made the Agen prunes which the French regard as the best in the world. They come from *prunier d'Ente*, trees grafted in a way learned by Frenchmen when on the Crusades. The most popular tree is called *Robe-Sergent*.

Though modern and very busy, with wide avenues, Gravier Esplanade is by the river, and riverside walks and the mild climate make it very pleasant. There is a huddle of old, narrow streets around the town hall and three old mansions from the 16th to 17th centuries have been made into an interesting museum with some fine paintings. Its pride is the Venus Le Mas, a Greek marble statue of perfect proportions which stands on a mosaic pavement, dramatically spotlit. It was dug up by a local farmer in 1876.

The Renaissance paintings include two very good head-portraits *Fair-haired Man* and *Dark-haired Man* dated 1550 by a painter called Corneille de Lyon – the only work I have seen by him. It seems that he came from the Hague in Holland, was naturalised French and was portrait painter to the French Royal family.

The 17th to 18th century paintings are delightful, especially two by François de Troy – *Judgement of Paris* and a portrait of the Count of Toulouse; Giambattista Tiepoli, the great Venetian painter's *Dying Page*; and a picture of the comtesse Du Barry by the 18th-century fashionable Court painter François-Hubert Drouais.

Better still are the Goya's – five of them, given to Agen with Spanish pottery and pictures by lesser Spanish artists by a local man, the Count of Chaudardy, French Ambassador to Spain. Two of the pictures show very different views of flying. 'Caprices' shows an elephant and a cow flying over a crowd of people who, not unnaturally, look terrified. The other is of the Montgolfier Balloon being launched from a Madrid park in 1793.

The 19th-century paintings are very good, too. Corot's 'Pond at Ville d'Avray' is one of this great landscape painter's best. There are several paintings by Louis Lebourg, one of the Honfleur painters with Boudin and his Ferme St Siméon Impressionists, and a room devoted to the 19th-century Romanian painter Nicolae Grigorescu, who specialised in painting peasants and was active in his country's independence movement against the occupying Turks. There are also several fine Impressionist landscapes, including works by Sisley and Labasq.

From the tower, which has a viewing table, you can see over the town to the Gascony hills.

Agen's cathedral of St Caprais has a striking 12th-century apse, but it was heavily restored last century – and has some 19th-century pictures.

TOURIST INFORMATION 107 boulevard Carnot (53.47.36.09)
MARKETS Wednesday, Saturday, Sunday a.m. 2nd Monday December: Goose Fair. Monday before Easter: Ham Fair. June: Pine Fair

HOTELS

Résidence des Jacobins (no restaurant), 1 ter pl. Jacobins (53.47.03.31). Attractively decorated; antique furniture. ROOMS D–F.

Corne d'Or, 2km NW by N113 at Coleyrac-Saint-Cirq (53.47.02.76). Old hostelry modernised; view over Garonne

river. Good range of menus. ROOMS D–E. MEALS C–F. Shut Sunday evening. Saturday; mid-July–7 August.
Rigalette, 2km N by D302 (53·47·37·44). Attractive; in park. Modern regional dishes. ROOMS D–E. MEALS D–G. Shut Monday; 24–31 August.

RESTAURANT

Absinthe, 29 bis rue Voltaire (53.66.16.94). Little restaurant with straightforward classical dishes and excellent value. MEALS A–E. Shut Sunday; middle–end July.

Montauban

[MAP 4, page 149]

Montauban has one of the most important and liveliest food markets of the south-west, which is hardly surprising, for it lies between the sheep-grazing hills of Bas-Quercy and the rich alluvial soils of the valleys washed down by the Garonne and Tarn rivers. Here are produced superb fruit and vegetables from market gardens, fields and orchards.

The market is held in the Place Nationale, a very irregular rectangle, with a market hall and a morning market when stalls spread round La Place into the double arcades of the pink four-storey houses which line it.

At each corner of La Place, at an angle, is an old, arched doorway, leading to narrow streets built on the standard grid pattern of a *bastide* (fortified village).

These *bastides* were started in the Middle Ages when living in the country was a hazardous business, with soldiers and robber bands stealing crops, stock, robbing houses, raping women and killing those who opposed them. To persuade people to stay on the land and work it and give them a chance to market and sell their produce, lords, landowners and kings had to give them protection. Also soldiers on the move needed a safe haven for the night.

To persuade peasants to live in the *bastides*, they were given a house inside and land outside to cultivate. They were exempt from military service and guaranteed protection – though *bastides* were taken from each other by the French and English.

The English started the idea under Henry II of England, but the French soon copied them. Both built *bastides* on the same plan of a square or rectangle with streets and alleys crossing at right angles in grid fashion, and a central square in which there was a covered market hall and covered arcades around, used as shops. If possible, the church was put on a hill. There were defence walls all round but the church was fortified as a last refuge if the enemy got through the wall.

Montauban was one of the earliest *bastides*, but it was not built by the English or French as defence against the other. It was built in 1144 by the Count of Toulouse at the request of the local people.

From the 8th century people started to farm in the area. A Benedictine monastery was set up on the hill at Le Moustier and a town called Montauriol grew around it. But the abbots of the monastery so mistreated the farmers and townspeople that they petitioned the Count of Toulouse for protection. He built the fortified village on the right bank of the Tarn. The advantages of freedom from the abbots, protection from marauding bands of soldiers and robbers, and the usual grant of land outside the *bastide* walls soon brought the local people flocking to the new town, which was named 'Mont Albanus', which became Montauban.

The arcades around the square were built in pink brick in the 17th century after fire destroyed the wooden arcade covers. They are roofed over with rounded vaulting. It is a superb square, but like so many around Europe, not improved by car-parking.

Take the west doorway from La Place and you reach the seven-hundred-years-old fortified church of St Jacques, with an octagonal brick belfry perched on a square battlemented tower. This became the cathedral after the Catholics took the town from the Protestants – the last bastion of Protestantism to fall in the Wars of Religion.

Montauban went over to Protestantism enthusiastically around 1560. The two consuls of the *bastide* were supporters of Henri de Navarre, the great, young Protestant leader, and encouraged the people to attack Catholic churches. Although Henri became a Catholic when he took Paris and was crowned King Henri IV, he made Montauban one of the four secure Protestant towns (places de sécurité) and reinforced the fortifications. Three big congresses of Protestants from all over France were held there. Many Scots Calvinists taught at the Protestant Academy.

But when Louis XIII banned Protestantism he sent an army of 20,000 men in 1621 under Charles de Luynes, his notorious favourite, to take Montauban. Three times the Catholic troops launched attacks. Each failed. Then for three months they besieged the town. The Protestants held out. Louis' army left. But in 1628 the great Protestant fortress of La Rochelle fell – a death-blow to the Reformation in France. Richelieu's forces took it when the relieving force from England under the Duke of Buckingham arrived far too late. He, as usual, was playing politics in London. After La Rochelle, a year later, Richelieu sent an army to Montauban, which this time showed no resistance.

St Jacques was raised to a cathedral and Louis XIII had the fortifications pulled down and pardoned the Protestants who were officially 'reconverted'. But that was not the way of Cardinal Richelieu. He billeted his vicious *dragonnades* on Montauban – thug troops given free range to steal, destroy, rape and murder, to cow all Protestants into total submission. As in many other places, their atrocities strengthened the faith of the Calvinists.

In 1739, the church dignitaries decided that they wanted a cathedral less fortified than St Jacques and built the vast, classical Cathedral of Notre-Dame which you can reach through the south gate of Place Nationale. Alas, it is an uninspired building. Unlike the rest of pink Montauban, it is white and cold looking, with two square towers and four colossal figures of the Evangelists which are repeated inside.

The one great interest in the cathedral is the large and famous painting of 'The Vow of Louis XIII' by Ingres, who was born in Montauban in 1780. The 'Vow' shows Louis offering his kingdom in the form of a sceptre and crown to the Virgin, who has Jesus in her arms. It is the epitome of Ingres' classicism.

A whole museum is devoted to Ingres' works. It is in the old bishop's palace, which stands at the end of the gorgeous bridge over the Tarn, Pont Vieux, which helps to make Montauban one of the most photogenic towns in France. The bridge was built in the 14th century entirely of brick and is 205 metres long. It crosses the river Tarn on seven great arches on piles protected by cutwaters. The arches themselves have oval spaces to allow more water through when the river floods. Originally the bridge was fortified, like Valentré bridge at Cahors.

The palace is interesting. A castle was built here in the 12th century to defend the *bastide*. It was pulled down in 1229. The Black Prince Edward, Prince of Wales, eldest son of Edward III, had a new one built in the 14th century during the Hundred Years War and in the basement which survives a room is still called the 'Black Prince's Room'.

The present palace was built in 1664. It was bought by the town when the diocese was suppressed in the Revolution, and converted into a museum in 1843.

Although Ingres went to Paris to study in 1796 when he was sixteen and spent the rest of his life in Rome or Paris, he left his own collection to his home town and Montauban is at least better off for his works than are the birthplaces of many famous artists, with thirty of his paintings in the museum and four thousand drawings.

Jean-Auguste Ingres was the son of a craftsman decorator. In Paris he became the student of David, who was deeply influenced by classical art. David taught Ingres that line was more important than colour. So Ingres' motto was that 'a thing well drawn is already well-enough painted'. He did at times stray from this ideal into gracefulness.

At twenty-one he won the covetted 'Grand Prix de Rome' enabling him to study in Rome. He stayed there twenty years, partly because he had quarrelled with David. He painted some of his famous nudes there, including *Baigneuse* and *La Source*.

The paintings he sent back to Paris were not always well received there. *The Vow of Louis XIII* was painted in Florence where he stayed from 1820–24. In 1826 he returned to Paris, and became professor at the Academy. Critics approved of his *Apotheosis of Homer* for the Louvre ceiling but they didn't like the *Matyrdom of St Symphorian*, which he painted in 1834 for Autun Cathedral, so back he went to Rome to run the French Academy. But Paris did like the paintings he sent back this time and he returned in triumph to be awarded the Legion of Honour and made a Senator in 1862.

Many of his works are in the Louvre. London's National Gallery has four.

In Montauban the most remarkable painting of Ingres' is *Christ Among the Artists*, inspired by Raphael. It is somewhat lifeless, but he painted it when he was eighty-two. The huge *Dream of Ossian* in monochrome was intended for Napoleon's bedroom. Ingres must have had some sense of humour or he would not have put the funny dog at Ossian's feet. The museum has also paintings by David, Géricault and Delacroix, who praised Ingres but whose own romantic paintings Ingres detested.

On the ground floor are some sculptures by Antoine Bourdelle (1861–1929) who was Rodin's chief assistant and has a whole museum devoted to him in Paris. He was born in Montauban. A painter and successful teacher as well as sculptor, he found influence in Greek art, but here his busts are outstanding – Beethoven, Rodin, Ingres, and also, in bronze, *Rembrandt as an Old Man*.

The Desnoyer gallery displays the major works of this Montauban painter (1894–1972). He was a conventional painter who appealed greatly to the French people and his works abound in museums and copies in provincial homes.

Do not miss the view of the river and old bridge from the second floor of the palace (Museum closed Monday and Sunday morning low season).

The 1870 War memorial on quai Montmurat is by Bourdelle. So is the *Last Dying Centaur* opposite the Ingres museum.

The N20 is not an outstanding road for scenery or interest but it is virtually the only route from Cahors to Toulouse and a stop at Montauban on the way makes the trip much more pleasant.

TOURIST INFORMATION 2 rue Collège Montauban (63.63.60.60)
MARKET Daily; also Marché au Gras (Foie Gras market): Wednesday, Thursday mornings November–February
FESTIVALS May – Song Festival; Mid-June – Trade Fair; Early July – Jazz Festival; Mid-August – Dance Festival; 1st week October – Agricultural Show

HOTELS

Hostellerie Les Coulandrières, at Montbeton, 4km on D958 towards Castelsarrasin (63.67.47.47). Very pleasant modern hotel built round garden and swimming pool in 7 acre park. Balconies or terraces to bedrooms. Roofed summer outdoor restaurant. Welcoming log fire in winter. ROOMS E–F. MEALS B–E. Open all year.
Orsay et Cuisine d'Alain, facing station (63.66.06.66). Superbly run; charming hotel with pretty soundproofed bedrooms. Good regional cooking by Alain Blanc (excellent local *cassoulet* of duck *confit*). Outstanding desserts. ROOMS C–D. MEALS B–F. Shut Sunday, Monday lunch; 24 December–2 January; restaurant shut 2–18 July.

RESTAURANTS

Rabelais, 13 rue Hôtel-de-Ville (63.63.21.09). Simple place to try true regional cooking (*pot-au-feu de canard*) at prices reasonable for city centre. MEALS C–E. Shut Monday.
Jacques Depeyre, at Brial, on N20 9kms S of Montauban (63.02.13.13). I loved Jacques Depeyre's cooking when he was in an old village auberge at Montpezat. Now he has moved to this all-new restaurant south of Montauban and has already gained

the popularity and accolades he deserves. He was trained by Guérard, Manière and Chapel. He has kept his cheap weekday menu and sensible prices all round. MEALS B–F. Shut Sunday evening (low season), Monday, part January.

Rocamadour

[MAP 2, page 147]

Rocamadour is truly 'breathtaking' – one tourist cliché which lives up to its reputation. The French rate it 'le deuxième site de France'. The first is Mont-St-Michel in Normandy. I would put them the other way round.

A beautiful little town, clamped to a sheer rock-face 150 metres high, Rocamadour keeps its medieval grandeur despite

Rocamadour

the souvenir shops, many restaurants and hordes of visitors. Stay overnight and see Rocamadour without crowds. See it with the early morning sun shining on rocks and stone buildings or lit up at night from the old hamlet at the top, L'Hospitalet. It is beautiful and awesome.

Below the town lies the gorge of the river Alzou. From the narrow main street of shops and restaurants, ice-cream parlours and 'specialities of Quercy' shops selling *foie gras*, *confits* and pâtés in fancy packs, it continues upwards by paths and steps lined with old houses, towers, churches and oratories, winding around rocks to the castle at the top.

Pilgrims used to climb the 216 steps to the oratory on their knees to plead forgiveness for their sins. Many were in chains. In the oratory where the hermit who founded the town is said to have sheltered and hollowed out the rock, they knelt before the altar to the Black Virgin and pronounced their '*amende honorable*' while a priest said prayers of purification. Then the priest removed the chains and gave the penitent a certificate and a lead image of the Virgin.

Many needed this certificate. They had been sentenced to make the pilgrimage by an Ecclesiastical court and had to bring back proof that they had done it or they would face prison or death.

Kings, lords, thieves and murderers went to Rocamadour. So did people called 'heretics' by the Church, such as the followers of the Albigensian beliefs – or at least any who had managed to escape murder by Simon de Montfort's 'Crusaders'.

Even today no one knows who the mystery hermit St Amadour was. Theories include an Egyptian hermit, St Sylvanus and even Zaccheus, publican disciple of Christ and husband of St Veronica. A 12th-century chronicler wrote that in 1166 a local man asked to be buried at the entrance to a chapel to the Virgin on the rockside. In digging the grave they found the bones of a man. They were placed near the altar and miracles began to happen. So they built the Chapelle Miraculeuse on the spot. This chapel was crushed by a rockfall in 1476. The present chapel was built last century – one of seven churches packed into the little Place St Amadour. Above the altar is the statue of the Miraculous Virgin (the Black Madonna) with Jesus on her knee, believed by experts to be from the 9th century. A bell hanging from the roof is also believed to be from the 9th century. It is said to ring of its own accord when a miracle is about to happen.

The pilgrims made Rocamadour very rich and inevitably it was sacked in the Hundred Years War by English and French soldiers and the freelance French barons with their private armies. Before that, Henry Courtmantel, eldest son of Henry II of England, plundered the church treasure in 1183 to pay the Army with which he was fighting his own father. He even took and sold the great iron sword 'Durandel', the sword of Roland. Henry caught a foul disease and died full of remorse in his house in Martel, falling on to the fire cinders in his agony. It is said that the ringing of the Miraculous Bell had made him flee to Martel in fear.

Rival abbeys disputed over who should own this rich church. Then in the Wars of Religion the Protestant captain Bessonies desecrated Rocamadour and laid it waste. It did not arise from the ruins and was extinguished in the Revolution. Then last century an astute Bishop of Cahors decided to revive the whole thing, rebuilding churches and restoring the town. Now some pilgrims do walk up, bowing the knee at each step, even if not on their knees. But they are heavily outnumbered by tourists. Two 13th-century town gates have survived, one crowned by a two-storey tower. The town hall is in a 15th-century house which was the *Maison des Frères* of the monks of Tulle abbey, which finally won the battle for control of Rocamadour against the abbey of Marcilhac. The town hall is open from 1 May to 30 September and inside you can see lovely tapestries of local fauna and flora by Jean Lurçat (*see* St Céré page 26).

The main street (rue de la Couronnerie) continues through the 13th-century Porte Hugon to Porte Basse, a delightful quarter with little houses running down the slope to the banks of the Alzou river.

Returning to Place St Amadour, the square of the churches, also known as Le Parvis des Églises. St Saviour's Basilica is in Romanesque-Gothic (11th to 13th century) and contains a fine wooden 16th-century figure of Christ. St Michael's Chapel is Romanesque with two very interesting, old, coloured frescoes outside.

The Treasure Museum has some valuable religious items, including crosses, insignia, sculptures and paintings, a 15th-century gilt chalice given by the scholar, poet and writer Pope Pius II, and two pietas from the 14th and 17th centuries (open 1 April–31 October).

The castle, which joins a 14th-century fort, was built last century on a cliff-spur. From its ramparts above a sheer drop are simply magnificent panoramic views of Rocamadour and the whole surrounding plateau (castle open 1 April–31 October). Below it are caves and the great cross of Jerusalem brought from the Holy Land by pilgrims.

TOURIST INFORMATION La Mairie (April–October – 65.33.62.59)
FESTIVALS *Son et Lumière* – nightly, Easter–15 October

HOTELS

Ste Marie (65.33.63.07). All hotels here are for tourists and compete strongly. My old favourite, recently totally renovated, is perched on rockface; lovely views from little terrace. Cheap. Six menus. ROOMS B–C. MEALS A–F. Shut mid-October–mid-March.

Beau Site et Restaurant Jehan de Valon, rue Roland-le-Preux (65.33.63.08). Old house in city centre. Good, young chef; modern regional cooking. Good wine list. ROOMS D–F. MEALS B–F. Shut 1 November–mid-March.

Vieilles Tours, 2km W by D673 at Lafage (65.33.68.01). Country hideaway from crowds in restored manor (part 13th-century). Regional cooking. Restaurant shut for lunch except weekends. ROOMS D–E. MEALS A–E. Shut mid-November–31 March.

Gouffre de Padirac

[MAP 2, page 147]

Nigel Buxton, the erudite British travel writer, once said to me: 'I dislike caves, but I would always return to Padirac'. It is indeed awesome and beautiful and the boat journey on its underground river is a joy. If you see a French guide book calling it 'commercialised', take no notice. It is inevitably highly organised because so many people want to see it, a tour round it takes one-and-a-half hours, and queues would be horrendous if the visitors were not conducted in an orderly way. Some of the guides *are* over zealous at hurrying their flock through. Perhaps they are paid by results or are trying to maximise their tips. The really unfit might puff and blow a bit climbing the stairs cut into the rocks. But the whole journey is well worth any effort.

Whatever the experts may say, everyone in the Loubressac area of the Gramat Causse knows that Satan himself made this

Gouffre de Padirac

great hole. The great ex-soldier turned evangelist, St Martin was plodding across the plateau on his mule, returning from a soul-saving expedition, when he met Satan returning to Hell with a sack of souls over his shoulder. Satan scoffed at the Saint's transport and suggested a bet. If St Martin could coax his mule into leaping an obstacle Satan would create, he could have the souls in the sack.

Satan dug his heel in the ground and made the mighty chasm. St Martin and his athletic mule jumped it – all 100 metres of it – a feat worthy of an equestrian gold medal. Satan fled to Hell by way of the hole he had made. And that frightened away many local people for centuries, though they did hide there in the Hundred Years War and the Wars of Religion. It seems that violent flooding of the underground river last century opened up a way between the hole and the underground galleries. The passage was discovered by the speleologist E.A. Martel in 1889. He made nine expeditions and in 1890 reached the Chamber of the Great Dome.

In 1947 an expedition proved by fluorescent colouring of the Padirac river that it reappears above ground 11km away where the Lombard rises and in rocks near the Dordogne at Montvalent.

The entrance hall of the caves, where you take a lift or stairs down the well, does look rather like a Victorian railway-station ticket area, complete with guide book and souvenir shops. Steps going down 99 metres are quite steep but you may have to queue for the lift.

Down there you walk along a gallery for 300 metres to the flat-bottomed boats. The boatmen hurry you along a bit in high season, to take as many people round in a day as possible, and off season with fewer boats running, the 700 metre boat trip is more enchanting. But at any time it is beautiful and unearthly. The waters are smooth and incredibly translucent, the passing rock-scenery is made even more enchanting by clever lighting. The only jarring note is the moment when someone on a rock seems to be firing at you. It is the official photographer, taking flash pictures of every passing boat. Unless you know that it is coming, you will look like someone who has just seen Padirac's brother to the Loch Ness monster.

The water's depth varies from 50 cm to 4 metres. Its temperature stays at 10.5°C which comes as a surprise if you dangle your hand in it, for you expect it to be colder down there. The air temperature is as high as 13°C.

The roof rises to 78 metres and at the end of the lake hangs the spectacular giant stalactite Grande Pendeloque (Great Pendant) 78 metres long and nearly touching the water.

On land again you take Pas du Crocodile, a narrow path between high walls to the other chambers. As you walk along wet paths and up and down stone steps, some steep, you will see a column 40 metres high called Grand Pillier, then a series of pools separated by lumpy rocks and at the end of the chambers safe for tourists, a waterfall 6 metres high.

On the way back is a lake called Lac Supérieur in rocks 20 metres above the river – a beautiful lake of emerald waters. You return in the boat, then walk along a gallery to the lifts passing the kiosk where you can order pictures of yourself in the boat to be sent home to you.

Unless you are very young and fit, take the lifts up. The cave is open from Easter to mid-October.

Stalagmites and stalactites

HOTEL

Padirac (65.33.64.23). Quiet, cheap, simple rooms; bargain ultra-cheap menu. ROOMS A–C. MEALS A–D. Shut early October–Easter.

St Cirq-Lapopie

[MAP 2, page 147]

The great castle in the Lot valley 29 km east of Cahors which was so strong and important through history has almost disappeared, but this stretch of the Lot river is one of the beauty spots of France and the old village carefully restored by artists and craftsmen is a delight.

Facing a semi-circle of cliffs, the village itself is perched on a rock-escarpment that drops straight down to the river. It is,

St Cirq-Lapopie

incidentally, pronounced 'St Sear' and is named after St Cyr, a child saint from Asia Minor, and the local lord La Popie who built the first castle in AD 960 over 1000 years ago.

There was a fort here in the 8th century when the Duc d'Aquitaine made a last-stand against Pepin the Short, King of the Franks and father of the Emperor Charlemagne.

In 1198 Richard Coeur de Lion, the King of England and Duc d'Aquitaine, tried to take the castle from the La Popie family and failed – a rare occurrence. It changed hands several times between the local lord and the English in the Hundred Years War in the 14th century. In 1471 Louis XI ordered the castle to be demolished. But the remains were still sufficiently important for the Huguenots to take them during the Wars of Religion and in 1580 Henri IV had all the walls knocked down under his policy of leaving no castles from which rebellious barons could attack the crown.

The La Popie family moved down the hill to the turreted stone Maison Rignault, now called la Gardette. It contains a museum of 14th- and 15th-century furniture, and some Chinese treasures, including lacquer work and a Ming period frieze (closed Tuesday out of season).

For centuries the townsmen were famous for wood turning, mostly of maple wood from nearby forests. They made bowls, buttons, flutes. Then from the 19th century until the First World War they made most of the wooden taps for wine barrels. Almost all the groundfloors of the houses were used as workshops.

Today the fine, old houses are packed close in steep, narrow streets, most from the 13th to 16th centuries. They are built mostly of stone but some of wood and bricks. Many have wooden balconies or Renaissance mullioned windows. There are only two woodturners working now, making souvenirs for tourists. But other craftsmen and artists have made a good job of restoring many houses and sell their products.

The inn, *Auberge du Sombral,* is a beautifully-restored old house. The hotel *La Pelissaria* is a 13th-century stone house. St Cirq-Lapopie has only 179 permanent inhabitants these days, compared with 1000 in the 17th century.

On a rock terrace overlooking the Lot is the 15th-century

fortified church, built for worship and as a sanctuary in war, with narrow windows, a squat square belltower and round watchtower at one corner. There is good view of the river from the church terrace.

A path beside the town hall leads to the clifftop where the castle stood. From here are lovely views of the village on the cliff-face and a loop in the river Lot. An attractive corniche road D40 follows the river NW to Bouziès and another crosses the river by a bridge, just past St Cirque and follows the Lot upstream many kilometres past Cajarc nearly all the way to Figeac. This is beautiful country for travellers and wanderers taking their time.

FESTIVALS Painting exhibitions in Rignault museum

HOTELS

Auberge du Sombral, place Sombral (65.31.26.08). See above. Straight regional cooking. ROOMS C–E. MEALS B–F. Hotel shut mid-November–mid-March. Restaurant shut mid-November–mid-March. Both shut Tuesday evening, Wednesday.

La Pelissaria (65.31.25.14). Charming hotel, restored with taste (see above). ROOMS D–E. MEALS (dinner only) C. Shut early November–mid-March.

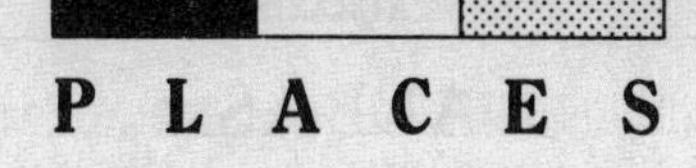

PLACES

AGEN

[*See* Major Towns, page 39]

AIGUILLON

[LOT-ET-GARONNE]

This lively little town is at the junction of the Lot and Garonne rivers. It was two rival towns which formed together into a *bastide* in 1296. Its ducal château was partly rebuilt in 1765. It is 30km from Agen NW by N113.

TOURIST INFORMATION 1 rue Bazin (53.79.62.58).

MARKET Tuesday.

FESTIVALS Fair biannually of regional products 1st weekend in August.

HOTEL

Jardin des Cygnes, route Villeneuve-sur-Lot (53.79.60.02). Hotel completely renovated; bedrooms modernised and sound-proofed. Nice grounds with small lake and swimming pool. Good value regional dishes with some lighter and more modern. ROOMS C–E. MEALS A–E. Shut Saturday except mid-summer; 2–9 April; 26 August–2 September.

RESTAURANT

Auberge des Quatre Vents, at Lagarrigue, 4km SE by D278 (53.79.62.18). Splendid views of the meeting of the Lot and Garonne rivers. 18th-century farm with rustic furniture and terrace with panoramic views. Known for good cooking of good quality regional products. MEALS C–G. Shut Sunday evening, Monday; mid-January–mid-February.

ALBAS
[Lot]

Beautiful village of narrow streets lined with old houses on the attractive left bank of the Lot between Cahors and Puy l'Évêque. It hit the headlines in 1962 when Princess Margarethe of Denmark married the local count Henri de Lamborde de Monpezat. In 1972 she became Queen of Denmark and he became Prince Henrik of Denmark.

ALBIAC
[Lot]

Village SE of Gramat just off D184. Several minor châteaux around it, of which the best known is La Pèze (16th century).

ALVIGNAC-LES-EAUX
[Lot]

Pleasant, quiet spa village on the D673, 7km E of Rocamadour, 6km W of Padirac. Very good centre for exploring this fascinating area, away from Rocamadour crowds. The spa waters are prescribed for disorders of the liver and digestion. The thermal establishment is set charmingly among trees by a pool. It is half-way between Alvignac and the village of Miers and is sometimes called 'Alvignac-Miers'.

HOTELS

Grand Hotel Palladium, route Padirac (65.33.60.23). Charming hotel with lawns and swimming pool. Best rooms in modern section. Hotel school, so rather formal, but good value. Rooms D–E. Meals B–E. Shut 15 October–15 April.

Nouvel (65.33.60.30). Modern, clean, good value for one-star hotel. Meals excellent value – regional and traditional. Garden. Rooms B–C. Meals B–E. Shut Friday evening, Saturday in winter; 15 December–1 March.

ANGLARS-JUILLAC
[LOT]

Another village on the lovely road on the left bank of Lot between Cahors and Puy l'Évêque. Church with Renaissance door. The Château de Cousserant is 14th century.

ANGLARS-NOZAC
[LOT]

On little roads north of Gourdon towards Payrac, it has a feudal château and an 18th-century château.

ASSIER
[LOT]

Galiot de Genouillac, François I's Grand Master of the Artillery of France, gave Assier two Renaissance monuments – the church and the castle. He was a very ambitious and ostentatious man, fond of displaying wealth, as befits a favourite of the magnificently ostentatious François I.

Galiot's motto, displayed all over the castle, was a pun 'J'aime fort-une' ('I love fortune' or 'I love one person greatly' – probably himself!)

Assier is just off N140 between Gramat and Figeac. Brantôme, the gossipy court historian, wrote that the château was built 'in a very ugly setting in rough, ugly, mountainous country'. But he came from a gorgeous area of the Dordogne. Now a lot of people love this wild part of the Gramat Causse for its calm and solitude. Brantôme did say that the château 'equalled in splendour the palaces of the Loire Valley'. It is difficult to tell now, because three wings were knocked down in the 17th century. The west wing containing the guardroom is still there. Friezes running above each storey show the legend of Hercules and a sort of potted history of artillery, with cannon balls and cannon spurting flames.

In a very unecclesiastical way the church, too, is decorated outside with a frieze depicting battle scenes. It goes right round the church. Inside the first chapel contains Galiot's marble tomb, with his figure in court-dress lying down on it. He is shown above in relief with a cannon and two gunners waiting to fire.

AUJOLS
[LOT]

Just off the attractive D911 SE of Cahors, Aujols has rather spectacular pot holes, old ramparts and a 12th-century church.

AUTOIRE
[LOT]

An absolutely delightful and little-known old Quercynois village with turreted manors and mansions, small half-timbered and old corbelled houses, with a fountain in a little square. It is on the little Autoire river, a tributary of the Bave, about 8km W of St Céré, and from the terrace by the church you can see the Cirque d'Autoire, an amphitheatre of rocks 2km SW where the river forms a series of waterfalls. Take D38 SW from the village, park the car in the Cirque car park and take paths to the waterfalls, cross the bridge and take a steep path cut in the rock for a wonderful view of the river, valley and village.

AUVILLAR
[TARN-ET-GARONNE]

Hilltop village, once enclosed, still with an old gate tower and curious but charming triangular Place de la Halle, surrounded by 17th to 18th century houses. In the centre is an old round market hall. There's a 12th-century house and ruins of a castle. The A62 motorway runs 3km S.

AVEYRON GORGES

[TARN-ET-GARONNE – *See* Gorges d'Aveyron page 91]

AYNAC

[LOT]

Aynac stands at the crossroads where the D940 main road south from St Céré is crossed by the very attractive little D39. Its old château is attractive and is in a nice setting of woods and fields. Its towers are topped with domes. The village has a 15th-century church which once belonged to Beaulieu Abbey.

BAGNAC-SUR-CÉLÉ

[LOT]

A medieval bridge crosses the river Célé here, just below the meeting of the Célé and Rance rivers. It is on N122 NE of Figeac.

BARBASTE

[LOT-ET-GARONNE]

Village with a famous fortified mill named after Henri IV who used it and so called himself *le Meunier* 'the Miller' during his campaigns. It was built on the right bank of the river Gélise, 6km NW of Nérac, in the Hundred Years War. The builder made the towers of unequal sizes, according to the height of his daughters. A ten-arched Roman bridge survives, too. Barbaste is almost joined now to Lavardac (page 105).

BEAUMONT-DE-LOMAGNE

[TARN-ET-GARONNE]

The Capital of White Garlic, known too for turkeys and equestrian events. It has an important garlic market in season on Tuesday and a turkey and capon fair on Saturday. The garlic is considered the sweetest and some of the best for cooking in France.

This Beaumont is 41km SW of Montauban on D928, in the valley of the Gimone river, and was a *bastide*. It still has a central arcaded Place for its markets and a 15th-century wooden market hall. Its 14th-century brick church with an octagonal belfry was also a fortress. Beaumont was the birthplace of the 17th-century mathematician Pierre de Fermat, who made discoveries in geometry and the probability of numbers.

MARKETS See above; also Garlic Fair in mid-September; Foie-gras market on Saturday mornings in December and January; and a New Year Capon Fair at the end of December

HOTEL

Commerce, 58 rue Marechal-Foch (63.02.31.02). Known for regional dishes and cheap prices. ROOMS B–C. MEALS A–E. Shut Sunday evening, Monday except in July, August; 24 December–20 January.

BEAUREGARD

[LOT]

Just south of Limogne-en-Quercy, between D911 and D926 on the very border of Lot and Rouergue. It has several old buildings, including a 15th-century market and Château de Labastide-Massat.

BEAUVILLE
[LOT-ET-GARONNE]

Beautifully-sited *bastide* on a spur surrounded by orchards and vines, with stone and wooden houses built alternately along its arcaded street. A small Renaissance château with a fortified tower. Gorgeous views. It is NE of Agen by D656 then the pretty D122 to the right, just across the Département border from Lacour (page 99).

HOTEL

Du Midi (53.95.41.18). Simple *Logis-de-France*. Very cheap. ROOMS A–B. MEALS A–C. Shut Monday evening; 1–15 September.

BÉLAYE
[LOT]

In a beautiful position on the lovely little D8 road which follows from the left bank of the Lot all the great loops and twists between Puy l'Évêque and Cahors. The little village stands on a hill with great views of the Lot valley from its upper square. It has an unusual 15-century church.

BONAGUIL CHÂTEAU
[LOT-ET-GARONNE]

On the very borders of Lot and Lot-et-Garonne, Bonaguil castle is a fitting memorial to the brutal, bullying Béranger de Roquefeuil, who in the 15th to 16th centuries turned a 13th-century château into an impregnable fortress. As an example of military architecture, it is magnificent, but hardly a comfortable place to live. Though mutilated in the Revolution, it is still very impressive. There is enough of it left to see exactly what it was like - a medieval castle built for war at a time when every other baron was brightening up or completely rebuilding baronial halls to make them attractive and comfortable. It was a powerful castle adapted to the use of firearms.

It took forty years to build, had 350 metres of walls and thirteen surrounding towers and turrets. Grosse Tour is one of the strongest towers ever built in France. It is 35 metres high. It was known as 'the Mad Château'.

Béranger de Roquefeuil was a thoroughly nasty character. He called himself 'the noble, magnificent and most powerful lord' and ruled quite a large area by brutality, extortion, torture and fear. When some people revolted, he built this castle to make himself safe. A mere one hundred men could defend it and withstand a siege. It was never attacked. But I wonder what Béranger would have thought of the musical evenings held there now in July and August? It is open daily 1 April–end September and Sunday in October, November and February.

BOUDOU

[TARN-ET-GARONNE]

This village on the N113 7km west of Moissac (page 116) has magnificent views over the Garonne and Tarn rivers where they meet and over the great St Nicolas-de-la-Grave reservoir. You can see it best from a promontory with viewing table south of the church. The foothills of the right bank of the Garonne have many vineyards and on the left bank are fields of crops protected by lines of poplars. The village 3km south of the river was the birthplace in 1658 of Antoine-de-Lamothe-Cadillac, who founded Detroit in 1701. He went to America with the French army in 1683. In 1711 he was appointed governor of Louisiana but returned to France five years later. He is buried at Castelsarrasin (page 80). The reservoir is used for watersports – sailing, canoeing, wind-surfing.

MARKET (St Nicolas-de-la-Grave) – Monday

BOUZIES
[LOT]

Just down the river on the left bank of the river Lot from St Cirq-Lapopie. A series of caves in the high cliffs were used by prehistoric man. The biggest is a Château des Anglais of the Plantagenet wars of the 12th century – fortified with a crenellated wall over the entrance with slits for shooting through. There are a number of these in Lot and Dordogne. They could be easily defended and were used as bases to pillage fields of crops or make quick raids on French-held villages. Bouzies is illuminated at night. The village has a church built between 12th and 14th centuries.

HOTEL

Falaises (65.31.26.83). Village auberge famous for authentic regional cooking. Remarkably cheap. ROOMS B–C. MEALS A–E. Shut 31 October–1 April.

BRENGUES
[LOT]

Hamlet next to St Sulpice in the Célé valley, on the lovely D41 road from Cahors to Figeac. It is perched attractively on a ridge.

BRETENOUX
[LOT]

Once a *bastide* (fortified village) built in 1277 by the Lord of Castelnau Château nearby, it is on the Cère river, near where it runs into the Dordogne. The riverside embankment is charming. A number of lovely old buildings survive from the *bastide*, especially in place des Consuls, where there is a turreted mansion and another old manor house through a covered alley. The covered market and the central square with covered arcades are absolutely typical of a *bastide*.

Over the river is Biars-sur-Cère, with houses grouped round the church on this delightful green stretch of river. It was a railway village, born at the beginning of this century to house men building and running the railway. Bretenoux still has quite an important station on the Bordeaux-Aurillac line, which also goes through Souillac, on the Paris-Toulouse line.

TOURIST INFORMATION Syndicat d'Initiative (Easter–15 September – 65.38.59.53)
MARKET Thursday
FESTIVALS Mid-June – Old Vehicle Rally

HOTELS

Bureau, Biars-sur-Cère (65.38.43.54). Real simple old-style *Relais* with pavement tables. Cheap, friendly. ROOMS A. MEALS A–C. Shut Sunday; 1 December–30 April.
Hostellerie Belle-Rive, at Port de Gagnac, 6km NE (65.38.50.04). ROOMS A–D. MEALS A–E. Shut 31 October–1 March.

BRUNIQUEL
[TARN-ET-GARONNE]

A spectacular and photogenic town on a sharp bend of the Aveyron river where it emerges from the Gorges d'Aveyron (page 91). The ancient castle stands like a sinister guard over the town which is very pleasant. Old houses line its sloping alleys and narrow streets.

Exploring the old castle, frightening views of the river keep appearing below you. The Knights' Hall was built in the 12th to 13th century. One of the river views is from a terrace near the chapel. In the main part of the castle where the lord lived is a Renaissance gallery with a pillared arcade. It looks straight over the cliff to a fine view of the river below. In the cliff-face rock shelters have been hollowed out. Though I have never been able to find out who made them, when and why, an easy guess is that they are from the Hundred Years War.

The bishop-historian Gregory of Tours (538–594) wrote that the name Bruniquel came from a fortress built here by

Brunhilda (567–613), daughter of the Visigoth King Athanagild, who married King Sigbert of Austrasia. Later she became regent to her two young grandsons, one King of Austrasia, the other King of Burgundy, and ruled half the Frankish kingdom. The other half was ruled by her sister-in-law and enemy Fredegond, regent for another juvenile King, Clotaire of Neustria. On her rival's death, Brunhilda took over Neustria and virtually ruled the whole Frankish Empire. Her cruelties were so intolerable that Clotaire and the nobles overthrew her. Her macabre death is famous. She was bound by her hair, an arm and a leg to the tail of an unbroken horse and smashed to pieces. The great square tower of the castle is still called after her. (The castle is shut on Tuesdays).

HOTEL

Étape du Château (63.67.25.00). Simple, cheap *Logis de France*. ROOMS B. MEALS A–D. Shut Tuesday evening, Wednesday; 1–15 February; 1–8 September.

CABRERETS

[LOT]

Delightful, beautiful and interesting village on the right bank of the Célé river on the lovely D41. Here the Sagne river flows into the Célé. Cross the bridge over the Célé for the best view of it. You can see Gontaut-Biron castle and at the opposite side the ruins of Château du Diable (Devil's Castle) are clamped to the fearsome Rochecourbe cliff like an eyrie. The English occupied this Devil's Castle in the Hundred Years War and came out from it to pillage the countryside. Now the village is tranquil and calm, with a charming old inn, Auberge de la Sagne, and one of my favourite hotels in the world, the idyllic old country house called *La Pescalerie* (*see* Hotels).

The Pescalerie Fountain is like a pretty waterfall which pours out of a rock wall quite near the road beside a mill hidden by ivy and trees. It is an underground river surfacing.

Château Gontaut-Biron (14th to 15th century) surrounds an

inner courtyard with a big tower on the corner. Its balustraded terrace overhangs the road. It is not open to the public, but must be a lovely place to live.

Grotte du Pech-Merle on a hill above the village is one of the most important and interesting caves in Europe.

In 1922 two boys (from a group of fourteen out exploring) found the cave's entrance. Inspired by the stories of the Cabrerets priest Abbé Lemozi, who was a caver and scholar of prehistory, they pushed bravely on, creeping along a slimy narrow trench cut by water. After several hours they came to galleries which must have seemed absolutely unreal to them. There on the walls were remarkable drawings of horses, bison, mammoths, strange symbols in red and black, human figures, hands, footprints. They told the Abbé, who explored the cave scientifically and called it a 'temple of prehistory'.

It is still believed that it was a religious temple of prehistoric man where he came to worship 20,000 years ago. The symbols seem to be the main evidence. But to a complete amateur like me, the drawings could simply be art – decoration to make those caves more attractive during dark winters and an expression of man's mind and heart. Either way, they are certainly impressive. You can walk along six big chambers joined through wide openings and along galleries for 1600 metres – over a mile. In the

Cave paintings

Hall of the Broken Column is a 7 metre frieze with black outlines of mammoths and bison. Galerie des Peintures is most impressive, with outlines of two horses, dotted, outline handprints made by stencilling around hands placed flat on the walls, and symbols. On the ceiling are women's figures. Prehistoric footprints are petrified in what must have been wet clay. There are bones of cave bears and roots of an oak which bored down to find water.

A museum (*Amedée-Lemozi* – open Palm Sunday–1 November) is also a research centre. It has interesting displays of bones, utensils, tools, arms and art works from 160 different prehistoric sites all over France, colour pictures of other decorated caves in Lot and Dordogne and a film on Paleolithic art.

HOTELS

La Pescalerie, at Fontaine de la Pescalerie (65.31.22.55). Enchanting country manor, superbly furnished with antiques and original paintings, 18th-century kitchen still used. From the flowered terrace where you take an aperitif, lawns, flower beds and trees run down to a river jumping with fish. The food is superb.

It is home to the two surgeons who run it – Hélène Combette runs the hotel superbly, with elegant grace. Roger Belcour still runs a medical clinic in Cahors but reappears in the evening to catch trout in the river, and to serve food and wine with energetic humour. He is an expert on Cahors wine and keeps a superb cellar. The old bakery is a lovely bar. A French guide book calls it 'Paradise on Earth' and '*La Quietitude*' – a perfect description. Even breakfast is heavenly. ROOMS G. MEALS E–F. Open 1 April–1 November.

Auberge de la Sagne, route de Pech-Merle (65.31.26.62). Charming old inn in quiet spot; lovely flower gardens. Excellent value meals. ROOMS B–D. MEALS B–D. Shut 1 October–1 May.

Des Grottes (65.31.27.02). Quiet, on river bank, swimming pool. Real Périgourdine cooking. ROOMS B–C. MEALS A–E. Open 1 May–10 October.

CAILLAC
[LOT]

Village on right bank of river Lot, with an old Romanesque church and two châteaux – Langle (15th century) and La Grézette (Renaissance).

HOTEL

Relais des Champs (65.30.91.55). *Logis de France*. ROOMS B–C. MEALS A–E. Shut Sunday evening, Monday low season.

CAJARC
[LOT]

On the attractive D662 road along the right bank of the Lot between Figeac and Cahors, on the borders of Rouergue. There's a 20 metre waterfall La Plogne, some fine views and, across the river, the site of a cruel Medieval legend. Take the bridge over the river and turn left along D127 (an equally attractive road). After about 7km you reach Saut de la Mounine, on the left bank almost opposite the ruins of Montbrun castle. There are lovely views from here. The name means 'little monkey's leap', from the legend.

The Lord of Montbrun decided to punish his daughter for her love of another lord's son and ordered her to be thrown from the top of this cliff. A hermit was appalled at such paternal cruelty. He dressed a poor little blind monkey in the girl's clothes and threw it over. The father saw what he thought was his daughter falling to her death and was hit by remorse. He was so pleased when he saw her alive that, the legend says, he forgave her. I hope that she didn't forgive him. The Lords of Montbrun were the Cardaillac family, who led French resistance to the English in the Hundred Years War. They also owned Larroque-Toirac (*see* page 102). Montbrun is in a beautiful position.

HOTEL

Lion d'Or (65.40.65.47). *Logis*. ROOMS B–C. MEALS A–C. Shut Saturday off season; 23 December–8 January.

CALÈS
[LOT]

The D673 west from Rocamadour along the Ouysse valley passes beautiful, wild, mysterious country with strange pot-holes where streams reappear. Nearby is an old fortified 14th-century mill, Cougnaguet, still working. Rounded arches span a loop of the Ouysse river in a pretty, green setting at the foot of a sheer cliff. Four millstones used to grind four tons of flour daily. Now only one is in working order and you can see it from early April to the end of September. Do not mix up this Calès with the one on the Dordogne opposite Trémolat, which has been done no good by the erection of a power station.

HOTELS

Pagès, route de Payrac (65.37.95.87). Attractive building with gardens. ROOMS B–E. MEALS A–F. Shut Tuesday in winter; 1–29 October.

Petit Relais (65.37.96.09). Pretty rustic inn with regional cooking. ROOMS B–C. MEALS A–F. Shut 20 December–4 January.

CALVIGNAC
[LOT]

Old village perched on a spur on the left bank of the Lot just west of Cajarc. Lovely river views. Traces of an old château and a number of dolmens (ancient stone tombs). Four km W on D8 is the spectacular Cènevières Château, clinging to a vertical rock-face. It is huge. The Tour de Gourdon, a 13th-century keep, altered in the 16th century, has great vaulted rooms and *oubliettes*, secret dungeons where you could hide captured enemies without even your closest neighbours knowing they were there.

A stone staircase leads to a fine Renaissance gallery and furnishings are splendid. The dining hall and main hall have great ceilings decorated with flowers and walls hung with fine 15th to 16th century Flemish and Aubusson tapestries. The views from the terrace over the Lot valley are lovely, too.

CAPDENAC-LE-HAUT
[LOT]

The ostentatious Galiot de Genouillac who built the château at Assier (*see* page 61), Grand Master of Artillery to François I, owned the castle here at the end of the 16th century but did not make it into a magnificent home and now only the remains of a rampart and a stronghold can be seen. It was one of the main Protestant strongholds in the Wars of Religion and after the death of Henri IV his great minister Sully, the man who actually succeeded in making the French pay their taxes, lived there.

The village is perched on a rock almost encircled by a loop of the Lot and is still attractive. Its narrow streets are lined with interesting wooden houses with pointed arches. Below is an important railway station and some industrial development, called Capdenac Gare and virtually a separate town. It is over the border in Rouergue. Figeac is only 7km N.

CANCON
[LOT-ET-GARONNE]

Very pleasant village on N21 19km north of Villeneuve-sur-Lot by an attractive hilly road with nice views to the east. Market, 17th-century château 8km NW, now an hotel (*see* below) and golf nearby.

MARKET 1st and 3rd Monday of the month

HOTELS

Du Golf, at Castelnaud-de-Gratecambe, 6km SE on N21 (53.01.60.19). Newly opened hotel with 9- and 18-hole golf courses. Club-house in an 18th-century manor. Very quiet hotel. ROOMS E–F. MEALS C–F. Shut 5 January–5 February.

Château de Monviel, at Monviel, 8km NW (53.01.71.64). Remarkable and attractive hotel made from the 17th-century Château de Rochemont perched behind its ramparts. Huge rooms with lovely views over the grounds; delightful swimming pool. Splendid service. Very good cooking by new lady chef. Reasonable prices for Relais et Châteaux hotel. ROOMS F–G. MEALS C–F. Shut 15 November–15 April. Restaurant shut Wednesday.

RESTAURANT

Hostellerie du Domaine de Valprès, at Lougratte, 6km N by N21 (53.01.65.56). Restaurant opened in 1987 in a mansion. Classical cooking, good value cheaper menu. MEALS C–D. Shut Wednesday, February; 20 October–10 November.

CARDAILLAC
[LOT]

An old village 9km N of Figeac off the N140. The Fort, or old quarter, on a rock spur above the village was the home of the powerful Lords of Cardaillac. Bertrand de Cardaillac fought for Pepin the Short, King of the Franks, against the Duc d'Aquitaine way back in AD 751. Twice the English took the castle in the Hundred Years War. Later the village became Protestant and was on the list of the safe Protestant retreats (*places de sûreté*) under Henri IV. But when the Protestant faith became illegal with the Revocation of the Edict of Nantes in 1685, the troops of Cardinal Richelieu knocked down the ramparts. It was reported that the inhabitants were all 'reconverted' to Catholicism – no doubt with encouragement from Richelieu's dedicated army.

Two of the castle's four 12th-century towers remain and some old houses. The Cardaillac-Lacapelle family still own Sagnes Tower and it can be visited. Two tall rooms with vaulted ceilings are reached by a spiral staircase. There are fine views over the Drauzou river valley from the platform.

HOTEL

Chez Marcel (65.40.11.16). Charming old inn; fine old country cooking (delicious *Causse* lamb). Good value, good helpings. Cheap rooms. ROOMS B. MEALS A–E. Shut Monday; 15–31 October.

CARENNAC
[LOT]

Most attractive even by the Dordogne river's high standards. Old photogenic houses with brown-tile roofs around the old priory where Fénelon, the great writer-priest lived. A delightful place. Many houses are 16th-century. The priory buildings were damaged considerably in the Revolution. The priory was suppressed in 1788 and was sold by auction in 1791.

It was founded in the 10th century and later attached to the powerful, rich abbey of Cluny. Fénelon's uncle was senior prior and when Fénelon was a student in Cahors, he spent his vacations in Carennac. When his uncle died in 1681, Fénelon was made commendatory prior. This was a sinecure given usually to friends of the King or powerful men who took the money and kept clear of the job. It was the cause of the disintegration of many abbeys. With the abbot or prior away, the monks sunk into a life of sloth, drunkenness and often lust. Fénelon did nothing of the sort. He stayed for fifteen years until made Archbishop of Cambrai.

Here Fénelon wrote *Télémaque*, the adventures of Ulysses' son, unpublished for years. When he was made tutor to Louis XIV's grandson, the Duke of Burgundy, he had it published as a tract. Louis was furious. He thought it was a satire on his court. Île Barrade in the Dordogne opposite Carennac featured in the story as Calypso's Isle, and the people of Carennac named it that.

Houses from the 16th and 17th centuries remain, but little is left of the priory except a tower, a fortified gate and the prior's house, called the Château, where exhibitions are held. One room has a lovely wooden ceiling with Renaissance paintings.

The Romanesque church of St Pierre has a fine 12th-century carved doorway. The peaceful cloisters have been restored. They have three Renaissance galleries and one Romanesque.

TOURIST INFORMATION Syndicat d'Initiative à la Mairie (65.38.48.36)

HOTEL

Fénelon (65.38.67.67). What else could they have called it? *Logis*. ROOMS B–C. MEALS A–E. Shut Friday, Saturday lunch low season; end January–10 March.

CASSENEUIL
[LOT-ET-GARONNE]

On a loop where the river Lède meets the Lot, 10km NW of Villeneuve-sur-Lot by D242, Casseneuil is an old town of brown-tiled houses, many with balconies overlooking the Lède and terraced gardens. An attractive little town, once a port for river boats, it is now a sailing centre. It also cans foodstuffs, mostly fruit.

FESTIVAL August – International Folklore Festival

HOTEL

Auberge la Résidence, route Villeneuve (53.41.08.08). Attractive two hundred-year-old country *auberge*; terrace shaded with chestnut trees. Simple, friendly. ROOMS A–C. MEALS A–C. Restaurant shut Saturday low season.

CASTELJALOUX
[LOT-ET-GARONNE]

A very busy little industrial and market town with small industries from woodwork to machine tools. It is on the edge of the great Les Landes pine forests.

Its ancient *bastide* was dismantled in 1621 because of the strong Protestantism of the people. Alas, it doesn't mean 'the Jealous Castle'. *Jaloux* comes from an old word *gelos* meaning exposed or perilous, which must have been disconcerting to the people in it. Casteljaloux still has several old timber-framed houses and the *mairie* is in an old convent of the Cordeliers. Chapel and cloisters are still there. A few remains of the château of the lords of Albret are now part of the municipal park. Jeanne d'Albret, a Protestant poetess who married the Duc de Vendôme was the mother of Henri IV. Sailing and canoeing on Lac de Clarens, 2km S.

MARKET Tuesday and Saturday.

HOTELS

Les Cadets de Gascogne, place Gambetta (53.93.00.59). Absolutely traditional old provincial inn on the main square where the Malvauds, once of St Céré, provide friendly comfort and outstanding authentic regional cooking. Lovely terrace-garden for fine days. ROOMS B–E. MEALS B–F. Open all year.

Vieille Auberge, 11 rue Posterne (53.93.01.36). Happy hotel with an old world atmosphere. Classic cooking. Cheap. Good value. ROOMS A–C. MEALS A–E. Shut Sunday evening, Monday; 1–7 March; 1–15 June; 15–31 October.

CASTELNAU CASTLE

[LOT]

You can still see the magnificent redstone pile of Castelnau Castle for miles around. It stands high on a spur above the village of Prudhomat where the Cère river joins the Dordogne, with the river Bave joining just a kilometre downstream. It is the most formidable medieval castle in France.

Built in the 11th century, it was extended in the Hundred Years War until it was 5km around its ramparts. The garrison was 1500 men with 100 horses. From the 17th century it was neglected. Perhaps nobody had enough money to keep it up! Much of it was destroyed in the Revolution and in 1851 a fire swept through the interior.

At the beginning of this century a tenor of l'Opéra-Comique in Paris, Jean Monliérat, bought it and, amazingly, restored and furnished it. When he died in 1932 he left it to the French State.

The site is a rough triangle, with a strong round tower at each corner and towers projecting from each side. Three perimeter walls around it still stand but the old ramparts have been replaced by tree-lined avenues.

Inside the walls stands the huge square Saracen's Tower – 62 metres high.

In the restored living quarters is a fine collection of furniture with art treasures and tapestries from Beauvais and Aubusson. In the oratory is 15th-century stained glass and a 14th-century triptych of the Crucifixion.

Perhaps the greatest scene is the view from the former ramparts and the tower. Northward is a panoramic view of the Dordogne towards Beaulieu and westward to the remarkable Cirque de Montvalent, north-east to the river Cère valley, south-east towards St Céré. Loubressac stands on its hill to the south-west and on the north-west horizon you see the remains of Turenne castle, hated rival of Castelnau in the Middle Ages.

From the 11th century the Lords of Castelnau regarded themselves as the strongest in Quercy and called themselves 'the Second Barons of Christendom', paying homage only to the Counts of Toulouse. But in 1184 Raymond of Toulouse gave sovereignty over Castelnau to the rival Viscount of Turenne.

Infuriated by such an insult, the Lord of Castelnau paid homage to the powerful Philippe-Auguste, King of France and enemy of Richard Coeur de Lion. A bitter war started between Castelnau and Turenne. When Philippe's son Louis VIII came to the French throne he decided in favour of Turenne, but it was a symbolic judgement which the Lord of Castelnau had to accept. Under it he had to pay each year to his overlord the Viscount of Turenne, just one hen's egg. Every year, with full pomp and ceremony, four oxen bore a newly laid egg to Turenne castle. Strangely the Vicomté of Turenne did not technically come under the French crown until a Viscount sold his rights to Louis XV in the 18th century.

CASTELNAU-MONTRATIER

[LOT]

A completely different 'Newcastle', SW of Cahors on the border of Tarn-et-Garonne. A hilltop town founded in the 13th century by Ratier, Lord of Castelnau, who gave it his name 'Mont Ratier'.

The previous village had been destroyed by the warlord Simon de Montfort, father of the English statesman, in 1214 when he used the excuse of a crusade against the Albigensian 'heretics' to loot, destroy or steal villages, manors, castles and land. Old houses still line streets, the main square is a listed monument and there are three windmills on a nearby hill. This Castelnau is 12km westward off the N20 main road going south from Cahors. The countryside produces superb peaches and a golden dessert grape called Moissac.

HOTELS

Arcades, place Gambetta (65.21.95.52). ROOMS A–B. MEALS A–C.

Trois Moulins (65.21.92.95). *Logis* with one more star than *Arcades* but food not quite so good. ROOMS C–D. MEALS A.

CASTELSAGRAT

[TARN-ET-GARONNE]

Another old *bastide*, founded in 1270, 3km N of the D953 road which joins Valence to Lauzette, NW of Moissac. Arcades and attractive old houses surround the square, which has a central well.

CASTELSARRASIN

[TARN-ET-GARONNE]

A thriving town of 12,000 people, 8km over the Tarn river S from Moissac, it is an important agricultural market, with a renowned poultry fair on the Thursday before Christmas. It has a large, brick, late 12th-century church and in an old Carmelite church is the tomb of the founder of Detroit, Antoine de Lamothe-Cadillac, born over the Garonne at St Nicolas-de-la-Grave (page 66).

MARKET Thursday.

HOTEL

Deux Mers, place Omer-Sarraut (63.32.30.88). Entirely renovated. ROOMS C. Shut Monday; first fortnight in September. Several restaurants nearby.

RESTAURANT

Saint-Louis, 1 place Omer-Sarraut (63.32.53.50). Classical cooking. MEALS A–D. Shut Sunday evening, Monday; early September.

CASTILLONNÈS

[LOT-ET-GARONNE]

A restored *bastide* of 1260 on a hill above the Dropt river, on N21, 33km N of Villeneuve-sur-Lot. The central square surrounded by arcades is absolutely delightful. 3km W are the ruins of old Cahuzac with a charming chapel of 1513 in the hamlet. Cahuzac is associated with Rabelais. Here the Duc de la Rochefoucauld, the man who dared to oppose Richelieu, wrote his Maxims, between 1653–62 when he was in retirement. He was entangled in a series of love affairs and his autobiography caused such a scandal that he said he had not written it! One of his mistresses was Anne, Duchesse de Longueville, sister of the great Condé and an active politician. Other lovers included Madame de Sablé and Marie, Comtesse de la Fayette, the romantic novelist and authoress of '*Zaïda*' and '*La Princesse de Clèves*', a vivid picture of court life in her day.

MARKET Tuesday.

CATUS

[LOT]

On D6 north from the Cahors–Puy l'Évêque road D911 – 9km from Mercuès. Fine old priory church (12th, 15th, 16th centuries) and adjoining chapter house with Romanesque capitals and sculptures. Old houses in rue St Barnabé. River Vert running through the town dammed to make Lac Vert on eastern edge of the town. Good fishing.

HOTEL

Terrasse (65.22.71.49). Useful simple auberge. ROOMS B–C. No restaurant. Shut 15–30 September.

RESTAURANT

Gindreau, St-Médard-Catus (65.36.22.27). 5km SW. MENUS D–G. Shut 25 October–15 November; part February, Monday mid-summer; Tuesday evening, Wednesday rest of year.

CAUSSADE

[TARN-ET-GARONNE]

Until the First World War, Caussade meant straw hats. All those natty 'boaters' which you see Frenchmen wearing in old photographs and in great paintings came from Caussade. I expect even Maurice Chevalier's *chapeau de paille* was among them. Alas, fashions are less elegant and the little town lives on a variety of light industries. But it still claims to be Europe's '*Capitale de Chapeaux*'.

Caussade is on the N20 NE of Montauban, where the D926 from Villefranche-de-Rouergue meets it, and is a pleasant, busy little town without being pretty, although the stretch of N20 NW through Montpezat-de-Quercy and on towards Cahors is one of the attractive stretches south of Cahors.

It was another of the Protestant strongholds and, like the rest, suffered when its craftsmen fled abroad from persecution. Some medieval houses, a 17th-century mansion Hôtel de Maleville and a 15th-century church belfry in rose-coloured bricks have survived. And it is a centre for truffles.

TOURIST INFORMATION 1 rue République (63.93.10.45 – in season)

MARKET Foie-gras market Monday mornings in January, February. Dog Fair 1st Monday in August

HOTELS

Larroque, av du 8-Mai (63.93.10.14). Daniel Larroque uses regional ingredients to make a variety of dishes from ancient recipes to those he has invented himself. Reasonable prices for good quality. Gardens, swimming pool. ROOMS B–E. MEALS A–E. Restaurant shut Saturday lunch, Sunday evening out of season. All shut 21 December–21 January.

Dupont, rue Recollets (63.65.05.00). Christian Dupont has rejuvenated his old hotel and also its cooking. Very good value. ROOMS B–D. MEALS A–E. Shut Friday evening, Saturday low season; 1–15 November; part February.

CAVAGNAC
[LOT]

Just off D20 Brive-Bretenoux road on the borders of Lot and Dordogne. Remains of interesting old châteaux and buildings, including a 13th-century tower and château of the Giscard family. The church is from the 12th century.

CAYLUS
[TARN-ET-GARONNE]

A delightful little Bas-Quercy village in a lovely setting on the right bank of the pretty river Bonnette, on D926 between Villefranche-de-Rouergue and Caussade. Overlooked by the ruins of a 14th-century castle, the old town runs down to an artificial lake. The main street, rue Droite, has many medieval houses, including *Maison des Loups* (Wolves' Lair) a 13th-century gabled house decorated with gargoyles in the form of wolves. The street runs from the once-fortified church. Inside is an enormous figure of Christ carved in wood in 1954 by a Cubist sculptor Zadkine, who was born in Smolensk in 1890 and died in France in 1967. He was greatly influenced by his friends Braque and Fernand Léger and developed a clever technique of using concave surfaces to reflect light. This statue is strikingly different. There are good 15th-century stained glass windows.

Caylus' old market is enormous for a small town, showing how important the town was. I am surprised that more travellers do not discover very attractive towns like this. But not many people explore Tarn-et-Garonne.

The roads N and NE from Caylus (D19 and D97) to Puylagarde are very attractive and the D19 S to St Antonin-Noble-Val on the Aveyron is delightful and joins the beautiful D958 alongside the river. There is some rewarding wandering to be done in this countryside.

Along D933 eastward from Caylus are lovely views from a hilltop, followed by a view of Cornusson Castle with many towers, on a hill over the river Seye valley. It is not open to the public.

HOTEL

Bellevue (63.67.06.57). Useful *Logis de France* with truly fine views. ROOMS B–C. MEALS A–D. Shut Monday; 15 December–15 January.

CEINTE d'O (CHÂTEAU)

[LOT]

15th to 16th century château with huge battlemented towers overlooks the river Célé valley from D13, 43km W of Figeac.

CIEURAC

[LOT]

Hamlet NW of Lalbenque and E of N20 at Le Montat with a beautiful, pure Renaissance château and well-restored windmills. Worth a detour from N20.

Here are the Haute Serre vineyards of Georges Vigouroux (*see* Mercuès) who cleared a hillside abandoned for a hundred years and makes some of the best Cahors wine. (Visits every day except 12.30–13.30 hrs; tasting; audio-visual in English. Tel. 65.35.22.55).

CLERMONT DESSUS
[LOT-ET-GARONNE]

A restored 12th-century *bastide* in a lovely position above the Garonne river just off N113 W of Agen. Popular with tourists.

HOTEL

At Tres Escales (53.87.21.45). Quiet, restful, simple hotel with a terrace overlooking the Garonne valley. Regional cooking. ROOMS A. MEALS A–D. Shut Sunday evening, Monday.

CONCORÈS
[LOT]

Where the N20 S from Souillac meets the D704 SE from Gourdon is a third tiny road which runs SW into lovely countryside D23. A charming road passing through peaceful farms and hamlets. It becomes D2 to Concorès, where old buildings include the interesting Château de Clermont. Its chapel-tower is especially worth seeing.

CONDAT
[LOT]

On the D20 Brive-Bretenoux road before Vayrac, a village with a spa source whose mineral waters were used for treating women's ailments.

CORN
[LOT]

Village in a beautiful position on the river Célé, west of Figeac on the D41. Château de Roquefort, old fortifications and dolmens (ancient stone graves).

CRAYSSAC
[LOT]

Very attractive views along the Lot valley from this village between D911 and the river. Continue on D9 to the river for superb views.

CREYSSE
[LOT]

Very charming village on the Dordogne river with nice narrow streets and houses with with old-style, brown-tiled roofs. Some have approach steps and are covered with vines. It lies between the charming D23 road and the river, E of Souillac.

A narrow lane leads up to an interesting very old pre-Romanesque church with twin apses from different periods. It is the former chapel of the castle which is now in ruins. An alleyway climbs to a terrace. The little square shaded by plane trees looks like a scene left over from the past.

HOTEL

Auberge de l'Île (65.32.22.01). *Logis de France*. ROOMS B–C. MEALS A–E. Shut 1 December–28 February.

DOUELLE
[LOT]

On left bank of Lot just west of Cahors – a very attractive stretch of river, with excellent views. Major boating centre of the Lot. The river almost makes a circle here. The real beginning of the Cahors wine country.

HOTEL

Vieux Douelle (65.20.02.03). Local auberge. ROOMS A–C. MEALS A–E.

DURANCE
[LOT-ET-GARONNE]

Yet another *bastide* of the 13th century – little left of the fortifications but one gateway and pieces of rampart. It is hidden away among pines at the south end of Campet Forest, SE of Casteljaloux. The ruined Château Henri IV was a hunting lodge of the Kings of Navarre, Henri's family.

DURAS
[LOT-ET-GARONNE]

The wine town with a 14th-century château, plenty of restaurants, wine caves, hotels and camp sites. It is in the very NW of Lot-et-Garonne, near enough to Bergerac for some people to regard its wine as from the Bergerac area (*see* page 14). The Côtes de Duras is quite a popular holiday area for open air holidays, with amusing midsummer fêtes in every village and much wine-tasting. Many French people stay on farms or in gîtes.

Duras stands on a great spur above a plateau and the valley of the Dropt river, with a background of hills.

The castle is really worth seeing now that it has been

restored. It was sacked in the Revolution. It was built as a fortress in 1308 but turned into a pleasant house in 1680 by the Duc de Duras. It still has a strong round tower and other troncated towers but its façade has lighter Renaissance touches. Inside are interesting rooms, including the old kitchens. Music concerts are held there, so is the annual music festival in August. It is open daily for tours. There are fine views from the main tower.

The old square of the town is attractively arcaded.

TOURIST INFORMATION Syndicat d'Initiative
(53.83.76.32)

FESTIVALS Foire aux Vins (Wine Festival) 7th July
includes induction of the Maréchalat des Vins. July –
Fêtes de la Madeleine

HOTELS

Hostellerie des Ducs, boul. Jean-Brisseau, route de Ste-Foy-la-Grande (53.83.74.58). Among the vineyards at the end of the town. A classic hostelry in its rooms and cooking, made from an old school and its chapel. Good value. ROOMS C–E. MEALS A–F. Restaurant shut Sunday evening and Monday except July, August.

Auberge du Château, place Jean Bousquet (53.83.70.58). ROOMS B–D. MEALS A–E. Shut Wednesday off season; 1–15 December.

DURAVEL
[LOT]

West of Puy l'Évêque, the hillside and terraces are covered with vines, the wide valley with fertile fields. Duravel is the first village on D911, past Puy l'Évêque. It is 3km from the river. It has an 11th-century church which was part of St Avit Benedictine monastery. Three saints are buried in the crypt – Hilarion, Agathon and Poémen. A small road climbs to the Château of Bonaguil (page 65).

HOTEL

Auberge du Baran, route de Cahors (65.24.60.34). Village inn, well run since 1985 by an English couple Roger and Letitia Washbourne from Bath. In the bar you'll meet everyone from the local vineyard workers to vineyard owners from Cahors to Bergerac. Traditional French cooking by Letitia. ROOMS D. MEALS A(lunch), B–D. Shut Wednesday; January–March.

ESPAGNAC-STE-EULALIE

[LOT]

Very attractive village with a pretty former priory surrounded by houses with turrets and steep pointed roofs. It is in a pretty position among cliffs on the left bank of the Célé river, upstream from Brengues (page 67). The priory was known as 'Notre-Dame du Val Paradis'. It was founded in the 12th century by the Augustinians, and in 1212 became a convent for Augustinian canonesses. During the Hundred Years War the cloisters were destroyed and the church knocked around. It was rebuilt in the 15th century and the buildings are now a school and a presbytery. Inside the Flamboyant-style church which replaced the 13th-century building are tombs with recumbent figures of the knight Hugues de Cardaillac-Brengues (died in 1342) and his wife, and of Aymeric Hébrard, the Bishop of Coimbra, who made the monastery into a convent.

ESTILLAC

[LOT-ET-GARONNE]

Village south of Agen, on D931 past the airfield and under the motorway. It has an historic château hidden among trees. Built in the 13th century, it was reconstructed by Blaise de Monluc around 1550. He is regarded as the forerunner of the great Vauban as a military architect. He also headed the Royal Armies against the Protestants.

FLOIRAC

[LOT]

A lovely village on the Dordogne near Cirque de Montvalent. 14th-century church and donjon; 15th-century chapel.

FONGRAVE

[LOT-ET-GARONNE]

Downstream from Villeneuve-sur-Lot (12km). Fongrave is a tiny river port joined by a little riverside road to Castelmoron. It once had a snob priory, admitting only novices of noble extraction, like Fontevraud, which was its mother abbey. The church has some excellent 17th-century sculptures.

FONTIROU

[*see* Grottes de Fontirou et Lestournelles, page 96]

FUMEL

[LOT-ET-GARONNE]

Industrial town NE of Villeneuve-sur-Lot on D911 road to Puy l'Évêque and Cahors, which passes through Cahors wine country. It has blast furnaces, foundries and workshops but is also a market town. Its old castle is the *mairie*. You can visit its attractive gardens.

TOURIST INFORMATION Syndicat d'Initiative, pl.G.-Escande (53.71.13.70)

MARKETS Sunday, Tuesday, Friday

HOTEL

Climat de France, place Église (53.40.93.93). ROOMS D. MEALS A–E.

GINTRAC
[LOT]

On a rock above the Dordogne on the delightful D30 left bank road just west of where the river Bave joins the Dordogne. 5km from Castelnau, it has its own ruined castle, Château de Taillfer (13th to 14th century).

GLUGES
[LOT]

Charming medieval village on the Dordogne just S of Martel at the foot of cliffs in a beautiful setting. An old road lined with old houses crosses the village. Follow this W to the D23 and turn right for a lovely route to Martel. From Gluges are superb views of the Dordogne river.

HOTEL

Falaises (65.37.33.59). Attractive old turreted house with pretty shaded terrace under vines. Classical country cooking. Cheap menus very good value. ROOMS C–D. MEALS B–E. Open 1 March–30 November.

GORGES D'AVEYRON
[TARN-ET-GARONNE]

The river Aveyron takes no account of man-made borders and passes in and out of the départements of Tarn-et-Garonne, Lot-et-Garonne, Rouergue (Aveyron) and Tarn in a bewildering way. The stretch north-east of Bruniquel (page 68), called Gorges d'Aveyron, is no exception. It winds through high rocks with superb villages like Penne (page 125) perched perilously above it, through wooded hillsides, to a valley floor covered with peach and apple orchards and meadows lined with poplars. From Bruniquel take the D115, then at Penne cross onto the D115B, a superb little corniche road which takes you within 2km of St Antonin (page 131).

GOURDON

[LOT]

Gourdon is one of the most attractive towns in Lot – and it is almost over the border in Dordogne. A very old market town, it is the capital of the green, hilly, very wooded country called the Bouriane, which runs west from Rocamadour and Payrac. You can see all round this countryside from the top of a rocky hill where once the local lord had his castle. The town descends in tiers. It is rich in history and full of old houses, most of which have been cleaned, as in Sarlat. It looks bright and pretty but I thought it had more atmosphere when their ages showed.

An esplanade has been built where the castle stood and from this you get superb all-round views. With the castle gone, the 14th-century church of St Pierre dominates the town and looks rather like a fort, with two square towers pierced by arrow slits and massive buttresses. Even its rose window is partly concealed by battlements. It was very much part of the town's defences.

The maze of narrow winding streets below include a delightful old street called rue Zig-Zag. Many of the old stone houses are medieval and corbelled, and have mullion windows and carved stone doorways. Some have turrets. The 17th-century hôtel-de-ville is in a fine square surrounded by arcades, and the market. It is at the end of the very medieval rue du Majou.

The ramparts have been turned into boulevards, forming a ring round the bottom of the hill. Here is the 14th-century Église des Cordeliers (a Franciscan church), now secularised and used for summer concerts.

The modern town beyond the boulevards inevitably seems dull after the lovely atmosphere of the old town.

Gourdon was on the French side in the Hundred Years War and was burned by the English. A lot of it survived though and it was rebuilt, but the castle was demolished in the 17th century.

Grottes de Cougnac, the caves 3km from Gourdon, are

known for their white stalagmites and wall paintings. There are two chasms 200 metres wide with a network of galleries. The first cave has three chambers with stalactites falling like rain from the roof. The bigger cave has a *Salle des Colonnes* with stalagmites reaching to the ceiling and *Salle des Peintures Préhistoriques* (Hall of Prehistoric Paintings) depicting goats, elephants, extinct long-horned deer, human figures and various signs (open Palm Sunday–1 November).

TOURIST INFORMATION rue du Majou (shut afternoons low season – 65.41.06.40)

Stalagmites and stalactites

HOTELS

La Bouriane, place Foirail (65.41.16.37). Attractive, nicely decorated, family atmosphere. Good value regional dishes. ROOMS D–E. MEALS A–E. Shut 2 January–15 March. Restaurant shut Sunday evening, Monday in winter.

Bissonnier et Bonne Auberge, 51 boul. Martyrs (65.41.02.48). Pleasant hotel; *Bonne Auberge* restaurant serves good traditional local dishes (*confits*, Quercy stuffed chicken, *foie-gras*, truffled omelettes). Good value. ROOMS C–E. MEALS A–E. Shut Friday evening except high season; 1 December–4 January.

GRAMAT
[Lot]

Gramat is a very likeable town, far more important than its size would make you imagine. Not only is it a centre for agricultural fairs and markets but also capital of Gramat Causse.

This vast limestone plateau with an average height of 350 metres spreads from the valley of the Dordogne near Souillac to the Lot and Célé near Cahors. It has some extraordinary landscapes ranging from meadow land to grey cliffs. Magnificent canyons break the grand horizons. Between the narrow valleys of the Célé and the Alzou, which passes through Gramat to the valley below Rocamadour, is the arid, almost waterless region riddled with caves and ravines called Braunhie, which is pronounced Brogne, rhyming with Dordogne.

Gramat, street scene

Gramat is a lively little place, used for shopping and business by people from a wide area. It has one of the best old traditional inns in the Lot, right in its main square called Lion d'Or where tastings are conducted in its large caves of Vigouroux Cahors wines.

There seem to be markets a lot of the time in Gramat. Apart from general markets in the square, there are seasonal sheep fairs, truffle markets and nut markets. There are some fine old buildings, especially in rue St Roch, and a watch tower. On Thursday afternoons between 15 June and 15 September you can see a display of dog-handling at the French Police Training Centre for Handlers and Dogs. D14 S leads to the Parc de Vision, a 40-hectare zoo and botanical park, with mainly European animals living in their own natural environment (open daily). The botanical park grows better each year.

Down by the river Alzou (reached by D39 SW, then fairly soon on to a little white road right), in the canyon of Alzou, are many abandoned windmills. Moulin du Saut is beside a lovely waterfall (marked very small on the yellow Michelin map, 75). This is a rewarding diversion. Gramat is only 9km from Rocamadour, so a good centre for staying a day or two (*see also* Rignac).

TOURIST INFORMATION place République (May–September – 65.38.73.60)

HOTELS

Lion d'Or, 8 place République (65.38.73.18). A real Quercy inn in a fine old building, and a 'temple of Quercy gastronomy'. A hotel since 1790, but the building is partly 14th century. The bedrooms have been modernised, the dining room made beautiful but the character has not been destroyed. Patron-chef René Mommejac, Master Chef of France, scours the region for the best local ingredients, using many old Quercy recipes. His meals are delicious. Superb red Cahors wines. ROOMS E–F. MEALS B–G. Shut Monday lunch in winter; 15 December–15 January.

Relais des Gourmands, 2 av Gare (65.38.83.92). If Lion d'Or is full, this is the next best place to taste real Quercy cooking. ROOMS (simple) A–C. MEALS A–D. Shut Sunday evening in winter; Monday except July, August; one week early October.

GRÉZELS
[LOT]

On left bank of Lot, 4km upstream from Puy l'Évêque, this hamlet has a feudal castle Château de Grézels, which has been partly destroyed and rebuilt several times. Now houses the medical foundation Joliot-Curie.

GRISOLLES
[TARN-ET-GARONNE]

Market town on the Garonne on N20 S of Montauban where N113 joins it.

MARKET Wednesday

HOTEL

Relais des Garrigues, on N20 (63.67.31.59). Simple *relais* in quiet countryside with gastronomic cuisine at sensible prices. ROOMS A–C. MEALS B–E.

GROTTES DE FONTIROU ET LESTOURNELLES
[LOT-ET-GARONNE]

Just off N21, 11km S of Villeneuve-sur-Lot, are Fontirou caves, with stalagmites and stalactites of varied shapes and colours, cleverly lit. Bones of prehistoric animals found here are displayed. A good cave to take children. The guided visit takes only forty minutes without hard climbing or walking and there's a picnic area and children's playground (open daily April–September; Sunday in low season).

Lestournelles caves are 6km NW near Ste-Colombe-de-Villeneuve. They have forming stalactites (same opening as Fontirou).

HAUTEFAGE-LA-TOUR

[LOT-ET-GARONNE]

Attractive old village 10km S of Penne which looks as if it has strayed from Tuscany. The Gothic church is a fine building. Its Flamboyant doorway is surmounted by a lovely hexagonal Renaissance bell tower. In the village square, shaded by plane trees, is an old *lavoir* (village wash-house) and there is a fountain by the church to which pilgrims used to come to cure their illnesses.

HOUEILLES

[LOT-ET-GARONNE]

Important village in Les Landes forest on D933, 14km S of Casteljaloux, centre and market for all the remote hamlets.

MARKET Wednesday morning

HOTEL

Le Maquis Landais (53.89.10.21). In village centre. ROOMS C. MEALS A–C.

LABASTIDE-MURAT

[LOT]

The tiny town of Labastide-Fortunière might have stayed in obscurity but for the son of one of its innkeepers, Joachim Murat, destined to be an adventurer and Napoleonic King.

Murat, born in 1767, was trained for the church, but preferred to be a soldier. He fought with Napoleon in Italy and Egypt. Partly because of his mad bravery and partly because he married Napoleon's sister Caroline, he received quick promotion, becoming a Marshal of the Empire. His leadership of troops and bravery remained a great asset to Napoleon. He covered himself with glory leading the cavalry at Marengo. He was made Duke of Berg and Cleves, and then King of Naples and of Sicily. The Bourbons, supported by Britain, hung on to Sicily but he took Naples and the crown. On Napoleon's fatal Moscow expedition he commanded the cavalry and, when Napoleon left the Army on the march back he commanded it.

When Napoleon escaped from Elba, he began a war with Austria, was defeated twice and fled to Naples, then France.

After Napoleon's defeat at Waterloo, he took some troops to Italy to claim the kingdom of Naples but was caught and shot.

His son Napoléon Achille Murat fled to the US, settled in Florida, married Washington's niece and wrote a book on American Government.

There is a Murat museum in the tiny inn where he was born – just a kitchen and saloon on the ground floor, mementoes in the two first floor rooms – a typical pub of the time.

The village is in a lovely area, with two attractive roads southward – the D677 and the superb little winding D32 which meets the D653 and Vers river for a lovely run to Vers itself and along the right bank of the Lot to Cahors.

HOTEL

Climat de France (65.21.18.80). I remember when the village inn was called *Auberge du Roi de Naples*! This is a 13th-century house converted by the *Climat de France* chain. ROOMS D–E. MEALS A–C. Shut 23 December–21 January.

LACAPELLE-LIVRON
[TARN-ET-GARONNE]

On the lovely little D19 road beside the Bonnette river, just north of Caylus (page 83). An historic little hamlet with a population of 150. In medieval times it was a commandery of the Knights Templars, but after 1307 it passed to the Knights of St John of Malta, who held it until the French Revolution.

A fortified manor house overlooks the river and there is a Romanesque chapel. Southward on the D19 on a superb corniche stretch of the road overlooking the river valley is the little pilgrimage chapel Notre-Dame-des-Grâces. Built on a spur, it has a Gothic stone roof and a nice sculptured doorway. There are some lovely wide views of the Bonnette valley from around here.

NW of Lacapelle-Livron is an army training ground, used intermittently.

LACAPELLE-MARIVAL
[LOT]

Just off N140 Gramat-Figeac road, an historic little town which belonged to the Cardaillac family from 12th to 18th centuries. The castle was built over four centuries – the massive square keep in the 13th century, the living quarters divided by huge round towers in the 17th century. A Gothic church, a fortified gateway flanked by a tower and an old covered market place make a photogenic group, used often to illustrate French travel articles.

TOURIST INFORMATION Château (in season – 65.40.48.11)

HOTEL

Terrasse, route d'Aurillac, near Château (65.40.80.07). Country inn run by local man; country cooking; private fishing in a lake. ROOMS C–D. MEALS B–E. Shut 15 December–15 March.

LACOUR
[TARN-ET-GARONNE]

Another picturesque hamlet on top of a hill, it is near the border of Lot-et-Garonne, east of Beauville, a beautiful village which is over the border (page 65). Lacour's interesting Romanesque church has a massive square belfry.

LAFRANÇAISE
[TARN-ET-GARONNE]

Market town downstream from Montauban on the Tarn, 14km NE of Moissac. It was a *bastide*.

From a terrace near the church there are splendid views of the river running between poplars and willows, and of the rich, fertile plain produced by the river sweeping soil down from the hills. These riverside poplars in France which look so lovely now were planted mostly in the 18th to 19th centuries to help prevent floods.

MARKET Tuesday

HOTEL

Au Fin Gourmet, 16 rue Mary Lafone (63.65.89.55). Good country *Logis,* with lots of choice of menus to suit your pocket. ROOMS C–D. MEALS B–F. Shut Friday evening, Saturday morning; 24 December–10 January.

LALBENQUE
[LOT]

Centre of farming hamlets south of Cahors just off N20, and one of the top six truffle markets in Dordogne and Lot (Monday from December–mid March). Two small lakes. Beautiful 15th-century church.

HOTEL

Lion d'Or (65.31.60.19). Simple *logis*. ROOMS A–B. MEALS A–C. Restaurant shut Saturday

LAPARADE
[LOT-ET-GARONNE]

One of the most extensive views in this part of the Lot valley from the ramparts of this old *bastide* on the river west of

Villeneuve-sur-Lot. On one side you can often see upriver to Villeneuve, downriver to the meeting of the Lot and Garonne near Aiguillon. Across the river you can see to Montpezat on the D13 from which there are also fine views.

LARAMIÈRE
[Lot]

In the SE corner of Lot near Rouergue border. A few of the buildings of the 12th-century priory remain on a fine site, near the church. Just over the border 6km E by D115 is the former Loc Dieu abbey – a remarkable building which started life as a castle, half feudal, half Renaissance, and was converted in the 19th century into the abbey 'Divine Spot', together with the remains of a Cistercian abbey. (Visits 1 July–9 September except Tuesday). Also a superb 12th-century church using different shaded stones from ochre to golden.

LAROQUE-DES-ARCS
[Lot]

A magnificent site on the Lot, with remains of a Gallo-Roman aqueduct which, on a three-tiered bridge, took to Cahors the

waters of Font-Polémie spring in the valley of the Vers. An old tower still standing by the river was a toll station, collecting payment from all passing boats. St Roch chapel on a rock overlooking the village and river is very pretty.

HOTEL

Les Deux Saisons (65.22.16.28). Modern but in delightful setting. Classical cooking. ROOMS C–D. MEALS B–E. Shut Monday lunch (high season), Tueday (low season); January–mid-March.

LAROQUE-TIMBAUT
[LOT-ET-GARONNE]

Take N21 S from Villeneuve-sur-Lot and turn left after 11km along the very attractive D110 and you reach this little village of Laroque-Timbaut which has some lovely old buildings. Around an ancient covered market on stone pillars are some old houses with roofs of round tiles, especially in rue du Lô reached by an alleyway under a tower.

LARROQUE-TOIRAC
[LOT]

This fortress overlooking the Lot 14km SW of Figeac, is clamped spectacularly to a high cliff-face. Built in the 12th century, it was owned for a long time by the Cardaillac family who led Quercy resistance to the English in the Hundred Years War, so inevitably it changed hands frequently and was much damaged. It was actually burned down in the 14th century but its position was so important that it was rebuilt in Louis XI's reign.

From the village church square take a path to a round tower built in the Hundred Years War as defence against artillery. The huge castle keep once stood 30 metres high but in 1793 was reduced to 8 metres (26 ft). It is pentagonal. The Romanesque tower alongside the main building has a spiral staircase. The upper floors have furniture and furnishings from the 17th to 18th centuries (open mid July–mid September).

LATRONQUIÈRE
[LOT]

Small town SE of St Céré by a lovely road through remote country (D30). Good fishing in Lac du Roc-de-la-France. Three hotels in a town of six-hundred people.

HOTELS

Tourisme (65.40.25.11). ROOMS C–D. MEALS A–D. Shut January, February.
Commerce (65.40.25.09). Simple *Logis*. Very cheap. ROOMS A–B. MEALS A–C.

LAUZERTE
[TARN-ET-GARONNE]

A *bastide* which you can see for miles from the hills and plains of Bas-Quercy, north of Moissac. It is lovely country, at the meeting place of several very attractive roads and among many small rivers. The one that flows down to it from over the Lot border at Montcuq is the Barguelonnette, which meets the Barguelonne about 10km to the SW, and that flows into the Tarn at Valence.

The *bastide* was built in 1241 by the Count of Toulouse and occupied for a long time by the English. It is a likeable little town whose greystone houses have almost flat roofs. They surround the church and the usual *bastide* central market square with covered arcades. Around the square and in rue du Château are old Gothic and Renaissance houses in wood and stone. Many houses are being restored.

Lauzerte is a centre for exploring the pretty villages of the Barguelonne valley and Quercy Blanc, named after the limestone hills. The plateau with flat-topped houses and cypress trees has a rather southern look, while the valleys and hillsides are rich and fertile. Every possible fertile inch of the hillside is used to grow Chasselas dessert grapes, tobacco or fruit trees. For a circuit of Quercy Blanc take D81 S, turn right along D16, right again on D2 at Durfort-Lacapelette, over the Barquelonne and Lendou rivers, which takes you back to Lauzerte (about 25km). There are some good views on the route, which is all attractive.

HOTEL

Quercy, Faubourg d'Auriel (63.94.66.36). Simple *Logis*. ROOMS A–B. MEALS A–D. Shut 24 December–3 January; week around Easter; 25 August–5 September.

LAUZUN
[LOT-ET-GARONNE]

The barony of Lauzun was made a duchy in order that Louis XIV could make his favourite, the Gascon soldier Antonin Lauzun, a Duke. He was born in the castle which is still there.

Antonin Lauzun (1633–1723) was a spirited young soldier who became very popular at court, especially with women, despite the disapproval of Louis XIV's mistress Mme de Montespan. He was ambitious and unscrupulous. He was sent to England to help the escape to France of James II's wife, Mary of Modena, and her son, James Francis Edward Stewart, when James II was driven from the throne of England by William of Orange. The son became 'Pretender' to the English and Scottish thrones and his son, Charles Edward, was the 'Young Pretender' Bonnie Prince Charlie.

Lauzun was given command of the French troops when James II invaded Ireland and commanded them in the defeat of the Battle of the Boyne. He overplayed his luck in 1671 by seducing Madame de Montpensier, a larger-than-life lady who was the niece of Louis XIII, cousin of Louis XIV, and commanded an army in the Fronde uprising of barons against the King. She was known as La Grande Mademoiselle. It was rumoured that Lauzun had secretly married her. He was sent to prison for ten years by Louis XIV. He returned to court in 1682, and was involved in novelesque adventures but lived to age ninety.

The château was built in the 16th century and you can see its very attractive façade from the grounds, but the château itself was temporarily shut in 1989. Lauzun built the domed pavilion between the old château and the Renaissance house.

The large Gothic church has an 11th-century tower and two beautiful sculptures.

Lauzun is in the very north of Lot-et-Garonne, just 6km from the *bastide* of Eymet.

MARKET Saturday.

LAVARDAC

[LOT-ET-GARONNE]

Little town with light industries on a terrace overlooking La Baïse, 6km NW of Nérac. It is separated from Barbaste (page 63) by a bridge across the river. Before the river was canalised this was the port where they used to load barrels of Armagnac brought by wagon from Condom.

HOTEL

Chaumière d'Albret, route Nérac (53.65.51.75). *Logis de France*. Cheap, simple. ROOMS A–B. MEALS A–D. Shut 2–17 October; part February. Restaurant shut Sunday evening, Monday out of season.

LAYRAC

[LOT-ET-GARONNE]

Layrac is southward from Agen on N21 after you have crossed the Garonne and driven under the A62 motorway, on the little river Gers. There is a fine view of the valley from place du Royal, which contains the church of Notre Dame consecrated by Pope Urban II in 1096. It was called place du Royal on the flimsy excuse that Jeanne d'Albret, Queen of Navarre and mother of Henri IV, stayed there in 1572, in a house which you can still see.

FESTIVALS mid-August – Historic pageant

HOTEL

Terrasse, place Mairie, 32 rue de Montfort (53.87.01.69). Outstanding regional cooking with individuality. Nice atmosphere. Simple rooms. ROOMS B. MEALS B–F. Shut Sunday evening, Monday; 1–15 October.

LESTOURNELLES

[*See* Grottes de Fontirou et Lestournelles, page 96]

LIMOGNE-EN-QUERCY

[LOT]

Along D911, 36km SE of Cahors, it is in a particularly attractive part of the Causse de Limogne. You will find junipers, lavender, white-truffle oaks and many aromatic plants and herbs in the maquis (heathland). There are dolmens and strange stone shepherds' huts with conical roofs called *garriottes* (or sometimes *cazelles*). It is the centre for white truffles, not considered quite so fragrant as black. One of the main truffle markets is held here.

MARKET Truffle market 1 December, 28 February

LOUBRESSAC

[LOT]

A delightful old fortified town in the Bave valley, west of St Céré, it stands on a rock overlooking the river's left bank. The D118 by which you reach it has wide views of the Dordogne valley to Castelnau. From the tree-shaded square in the lower part of Loubressac are good views of the Bave valley and St Céré. But the best is looking north from the castle terrace – a tremendous view with the red castle of Castelnau standing threateningly over the meeting of the Cère, Bave and Dordogne rivers.

The narrow streets of the town wind up to the steep spur on which the castle stands. The medieval fort which once stood here has gone. The present château with a watch tower dates from the early 15th century but was converted into what is really a manor house. It became a farm belonging to a Napoleonic general. At the beginning of this century, Henri Lavedan of the Académie Française restored it.

Downhill is the hamlet of La Pougade. Turn left on D14 and on the right is a monument to the day when Allied aircraft dropped 100 tons of arms for the French Resistance – 14 July 1944. And each parachute was flying the French tricolour.

HOTEL

Lou Cantou (65.38.20.58). Good *Logis*. ROOMS C–D. MEALS A–D. Shut Monday; 30 October–15 November; 1–15 February.

LUZECH
[LOT]

The Lot loops so dramatically at Luzech that the neck of land is only 200 metres across. Once a canal ran through it, so that boats between Puy l'Évêque and Cahors were saved a detour. Now a dam has made a reservoir just upstream.

The town is topped by the 12th-century keep of a ruined castle which was held in 1118 by Richard Coeur de Lion. It was important enough to be the seat of one of the four baronies of Quercy. The English tried many times to take it in the Hundred Years War but failed. So did the Protestants in the Wars of Religion. Old houses remain along alleys running into rue du Barry-del-Valat. Houses in rue des Balcons are unusual. The town has light industries now.

On a hill to the north is a site called Impernal. Excavations show that it was inhabited in prehistoric times, then by the Gauls and Romans. Château de Caix lies upstream on the right bank of the Lot.

HOTEL

L'Île, rue Dubarry (65.20.10.09). Good *Logis*. ROOMS C–D. MEALS A–D. Shut 15–30 June.

MARCILHAC-SUR-CÉLÉ

[LOT]

Another lovely spot in the Célé river valley, about halfway between Cahors and Figeac. It is set in the centre of an amphitheatre of cliffs.

Abbey at Marcilhac

It has fine old houses but is visited mostly for its former Benedictine Abbey, one of those buildings the French call *belles ruines* (beautiful ruins).

Marcilhac Abbey was set up in the 11th century. It controlled the little sanctuary of Rocamadour but did not think it important and let it run to ruin. Monks from Tulle Abbey 'squatted' in the sanctuary.

In 1166 the body purported to be that of St Amadour was found (*see* Rocamadour, page 49) and the miracles started. Spotting the fame and fortune that might follow, the monks of Marcilhac threw out their brothers of Tulle. The Abbot of Tulle sent his monks to throw out the men of Marcilhac.

An unholy row had started. Lawsuits began. The Bishop of Cahors, the Archbishop of Bourges, even the Pope were asked to judge but none would give judgement. The argument went on for a hundred years. Finally the brethren of Tulle bribed their brothers of Marcilhac to give up their claim.

Marcilhac was extremely prosperous until the Hundred Years War, when English and French army pillagers almost destroyed it. After the Reformation, the Hébrard family, who controlled the Célé valley (*see* St Sulpice) took it over and it finally disappeared during the Revolution.

You can see the early Romanesque part of the Abbey, open to the sky, with a tall square tower and religious carvings, and the almost separate 15th-century Gothic part, Flamboyant in style. This is in use as a church after rebuilding. The chapel is decorated with wood carvings of episodes in the life of Christ.

A corniche road overlooking the Célé valley with steep hairpin bends takes you to Grotte de Bellevue – not the most spectacular cave in Lot but one of the prettiest. The coral-shaped concretions are dark red from iron-oxide in the rock or are of shining white calcite (crystalized calcium carbonate). Some of the stalactites hanging from the roof are quite grotesque and the delicately thin stalagmites rise from the floor like spikes. Hercules Column rises 4 metres from floor to ceiling and is 3.5 metres round (open daily from Spring holidays until 30 September, Sunday only in November).

MARMANDE
[LOT-ET-GARONNE]

Where the famous, big, curvaceous tomatoes come from. Buy the seeds in France and grow them outdoors in England – well, the south, anyway. I grew 700 lbs one year in my Kent garden! They used to call them *pommes d'amour* because they were supposed to help lovers. Try the local clear plum and pear brandies.

It's a true market town for plums, peaches, melons, tobacco, tomatoes, with a lively cattle market some Saturdays.

The landscape around here is often compared with Tuscany in Italy. From the cloisters of the church of Notre Dame are splendid views of the Garonne river winding through the plain. The church is partly 13th-century.

TOURIST INFORMATION boulevard Gambetta (53.64.32.50).
MARKETS Monday, Thursday, Saturday
FESTIVALS April–May – Cavalcade du Marmandais.
Spring – Printemps Musical.

HOTELS

Capricorne, route d'Agen (53.64.16.14). Motel; modern, comfortable, swimming pool. Restaurant separately owned. ROOMS C–D. MEALS A–F. Shut 22 December–7 January. Restaurant shut Sunday except evening June–October.

Auberge de Guyenne, 9 rue Martignac (53.64.01.77). Good classical regional cooking – the real thing. ROOMS A–D. MEALS A–E. Shut Sunday evening, Monday low season; 2 January–2 February.

RESTAURANT

Thierry Arbeau, 10 av Christian Baylac (53.64.24.03). Interesting variety of dishes by young chef, with emphasis on regional. Cheaper menu is splended value. Attractive building. MEALS C–E. Shut Sunday evening, Monday.

Auberge du Moulin d'Ané, at Virazeil, 4km E, route de Gontaud by D933 and D267 (53.20.18.25). Beautiful little old mill by the tiny river Trec with a terrace overlooking a waterfall and winter-garden. Good cooking. MEALS B–F. Shut part February; 16 August–5 September.

MARTEL
[Lot]

History was changed in this handsome, likeable town, built mostly of golden Quercy stone.

In the 8th century the Saracens – the great Mohammedan warriors – had come through Spain and over the Pyrénées as far as Poitiers, in their quest to conquer Europe. Charles Martel, Duke of the Franks, known as 'the Hammer of God', defeated their armies near Poitiers in 732, pursued them into Aquitaine and a few years later defeated them again here and drove them out of France. At the scene of the battle he had a church built. A town grew up around it and they called it Martel after its founder and took as its crest three hammers, the weapon he used in battle.

In the 12th century Henry Courtmantel, son and heir of Henry II, King of England, who was making war on his father, fled here after robbing the Holy Shrine at Rocamadour (*see* page 49).

Covered market, Martel

He was very sick and believed it was God's punishment. He confessed his crimes and messengers sought out Henry II and begged him to come and forgive his son on his death-bed. Henry II was at the siege of Limoges and sent a messenger with his pardon. The messenger returned and found Henry dying, deserted by his followers, and fallen on a bed of hot cinders in agony. Maison Fabri, an old mansion flanked by a round tower to the south of Place des Consuls, is said to be the house where he died.

The old town's perimeter walls have made way for boulevards, but towers and gateways remain from the Medieval fortifications.

The Gothic church of St Maur has two watch towers, and a main bay topped with a line of battlements. Its belfry is 48 metres high and has narrow loopholes for firing through. In fact the church was once also a fortress. Beneath its porch is a superb Romanesque tympanum of the Last Judgement.

The rue Droite, which leads to the Place des Consuls, the main square, is lined with old houses. In the square itself are some fine old mansions, including Hôtel de la Raymondie which belonged to the Turenne family. It was started in 1280. There's a crenellated belfry, a tower at each corner and rose windows facing into the courtyard. It is now the town hall and tourist office. In the centre of the square is the old covered market with roof resting on stone square pillars. It is a great market centre for truffles and nuts. Another fine mansion is the 16th to 17th-century Hôtel de Chauffour on the west side of the square.

Alongside Hôtel Raymondie is a small street containing many more fine old houses including the 13th-century Hôtel de la Monnaie.

TOURIST INFORMATION Hôtel de Ville, Place des Consuls (65.37.30.03)

MARKETS Twice weekly: Foire de la Noix (Nut Fair); Easter Saturday, Sunday and Monday

FESTIVALS July–August – Musical soirées; Early September – Festival of Poetry

HOTELS

Le Turenne, Restaurant Le Quercy (65.37.30.30). Two typical gold stone Quercy houses converted into an hotel restaurant underrated by French guides, who ignore it, to our advantage. Campastie family have cooked, father to son, since 1856. ROOMS A–D. MEALS A–E. Shut 1 December–end February.

MARTIGNAC
[LOT]

This village 4km north of Puy-l'Évêque on tiny roads has a beautiful little rustic church in golden stone topped with a tall wooden belfry. The nave and chancel have most interesting 15th-century wall paintings. They are mostly in ochre and yellow and the drawing is simple. In the nave, a nobleman sitting on a man's back portrays sloth. One with a ham in his arms is gluttony. A woman riding a goat is said to be lust. Opposite is another fresco showing the Coronation of the Virgin and the Chosen being guided to Paradise by St Michael and being received at the Heavenly Gates by St Peter. There are other Biblical scenes by the chancel.

LE MAS-D'AGENAIS
[LOT-ET-GARONNE]

15km S of Marmande on the Canal Latéral de Garonne. Once a Roman town, it was here at Revenac in 1876 that a farmer dug up the Venus du Mas, now in the Beaux Arts museum in Agen.

The 12th-century church has a Crucifixion by Rembrandt, an early work dated 1631. You can see it by applying to the curé. The choir stalls with 16th-century sculptures are very beautiful.

Alongside the church is a 16th-century market hall.

MARKET Second Thursday of each month

MAYRINHAC-LENTOUR

[LOT]

Important little market town to the right of D940 going S from St Céré. Attractive fountain of Bonnefons, from Gallic-Roman days. Ruins of the once-important Château de Noailles. Markets on Monday, Wednesday and Friday, particularly for plums in season.

MERCUÈS

[LOT]

From the 12th century the Bishops of Cahors lived in this stunning part-Renaissance, part-Medieval fortified castle with four dunce's-hat turrets. Now it has been made into an expensive but absolutely delightful hotel by winemaker Georges Vigouroux. The terrace is a special delight, the views from it are magnificent. At the entrance gates but in the grounds, the old castle cellars under rocks have been put to splendid use by Georges, who is a grower and *négociant* (merchant). Here he matures his own wine from Château Haute Serre and others, sells wine, offers free tastings and has built an attractive hall for seminars and banquets.

The Hôtel is beautifully furnished and, despite the size of most of the beautiful bedrooms and the medieval-castle solidness of the building, it has a warm, comfortable atmosphere.

To find Mercuès, take D911 NW from Cahors for 5km to a tiny road on the right, signposted, which climbs up through a village and woods to the castle.

HOTEL

Château de Mercuès (65.20.00.01). ROOMS G. MEALS E–F. Open Easter–1 November.

MEYRONNE
[LOT]

Down river from Creysse on the Dordogne. Village built picturesquely into cliffs by a bridge. Caves in the cliff. The village church is 14th century.

MÉZIN
[LOT-ET-GARONNE]

Village 13km SW of Nérac. Here you can hire horse-drawn caravans or go on group tours across country by camel – following the forest tracks across Les Landes. It was Napoleon III who dreamed up the idea of camel breeding on the sand dunes of Les Landes. You stay in touring gîtes. Apply Les Attelages d'Armagnac, Domaine de Cézaou, 47170 Mézin.

HOTEL

Relais de Gascogne (53.65.79.88). Old hotel renovated and extended. Functional rooms. Very good choice of menus at reasonable prices – gastronomic and regional dishes. ROOMS B–F. MEALS A–E. Shut Monday evening; February.

MOIRAX
[LOT-ET-GARONNE]

Old fortified village 10km S of Agen with a beautiful and interesting 11th to 12th-century clean-lined Romanesque church, with unusual 17th-century choir stalls and panelling.

MOISSAC
[TARN-ET-GARONNE]

The 11th-century cloisters of the old abbey at Moissac are architectural gems of France. Their graceful arches and elegant columns are so beautiful that I wish sometimes that I had been one of the Medieval monks who strolled among them each day. Yet they were nearly knocked down just over a hundred years ago. Only a huge national outcry forced the officials to save

Abbey at Moissac

them from destruction by a railway company who wanted to run the main line to Montauban through them. But it is not only for the abbey that Moissac is revered all over France. It is also for the golden dessert grape, the chasselas, sweet and scented – called here the chasselas de Moissac or just the Moissac. The vines grow on the hillsides of Bas-Quercy and the Agenais over the border in Lot-et-Garonne, right down to the banks of the Tarn and Garonne rivers between Agen and Montauban.

The abbey was founded in the 7th century by a Benedictine monk from St Wandrille in Normandy. It was plundered by Arabs, Normans and central European invading tribes until 1047, when the famous Abbot of the great and powerful Abbey of Cluny, St Odilon, happened to be passing and took it under Cluny's protective wing.

It was sacked again when the abominable Simon de Montfort (senior) besieged Moissac in 1212. Raymond VII, Count of Toulouse, rescued it in 1222 and the Church celebrated by burning 210 heretics there under the Inquisition in 1234. The English took it twice during the Hundred Years War and the Protestants took it and desecrated it in the 16th-century Wars of Religion. Perhaps the life of the monks in those beautiful cloisters was not so peaceful!

The abbey was secularised in 1628 and suppressed completely in the Revolution.

The cloisters surround a spacious close. The beautifully-proportioned pillars of the long galleries are alternately single and paired, and are faced in varying tints of marble – white, pink, grey and green. The ornamented square capitals are exquisitely carved with scenes from the life of Christ, the miracles which he performed, his parables and the Apocalypse, with events in the lives of various saints.

A huge, very old cedar stands in the middle of the close. I cannot resist wondering who planted it and when.

Beside the entrance, a staircase leads to a vestibule from which you have a good upper view of the cloisters. In four chapels off the east gallery is a little museum with a collection of 11th to 13th-century stone carvings and photographs showing the way Moissac-style of Romanesque sculpture spread through Quercy.

The other Romanesque masterpiece is the south doorway to the abbey church of St-Pierre, carved between 1100 and 1130 by sculptors of the Toulouse school, responsible also for superb sculptures in the churches of Cahors and Carennac. The tympanum – the lintel and the panel across the top archway of the door – is magnificent. It shows Paul's vision of the Apocalypse, with Christ surrounded by symbols of the four evangelists. St Matthew is a winged young man, St Mark is a lion, St Luke is a bull and St John is an eagle. The Old Men of the Apocalypse look suitably overawed. St Peter, patron of the abbey, and Isaiah are on two side piers, which have a Moorish look, possibly because Moissac was an overnight stop for pilgrims on a much frequented but dangerous route to Santiago de Compostela. This whole area was under invading Moors until Charles Martel drove them out by beating them at Poitiers in 732. Historic scenes on either side of the piers include the Flight into Egypt. On the left are scenes of Hell's damnation, with a miser and an adultress being tortured by demons, and the story of the rich man feasting while the poor man is dying of hunger as his soul is carried away by an angel.

The other remnant of the 11th-century church is the belfry tower fortified for defence. A dome fell in the 15th century and half-destroyed the stone Romanesque church. Rebuilding was done in brick in Gothic style. The inside decorations feature another Flight into Egypt from the 15th century – rather odd when you remember that the French had been persecuting and driving out the Jews since Louis-Philippe's reign in the 13th century.

Moissac itself has been called 'dull' by French guides. I find it a pleasant, quiet little provincial town among the vines of the Moissac hills and orchards of the Tarn valley, going about its business calmly without rushing madly into the 'French Technological Revolution' as some French towns have done, to the detriment of their environment and way of life. There are some nice 17th- to 18th-century houses around the abbey and good views from the tower. The church of St Martin, with 15th-century murals, goes back to the 7th century and is built on the site of a Gallo-Roman villa.

The museum in the former abbot's house has a 17th-century

staircase and rooms with folklore collections, including interesting old furniture, a very interesting 19th-century Bas-Quercy kitchen, and traditional Moissac *coiffes* (head-dresses). The museum is shut on Tuesday and Sunday morning.

How can a town which organises a *Festival Amateur du Rire* be dull? This takes place in June and if you like a good laugh, that must be the time to go. It is also a centre for sailing and canoeing, and the watersports of St Nicolas-de-la-Grave reservoir are only 5km down river.

TOURIST INFORMATION 1 place Durand-de-Bredon (63.04.01.85 – shut mornings low season).

FESTIVALS June – Festival Amateur du Rire; August – Fête de l'Été; September – Chasselas Grape Fête

HOTELS

Pont-Napoléon, 2 allée Montebello (63.04.01.55). Pleasant terrace overlooking Tarn near the bridge. Two good menus and regional specialities. Bedrooms overlook leafy quay. ROOMS C–D. MEALS B–F. Shut Monday evening except midsummer, Tuesday; 5 January–5 February; 5–20 June.

Moulin de Moissac, place Moulin (63.04.03.55). Quiet, very comfortable, attractive. ROOMS C–G. MEALS C–F.

Poste, 2 pl Liberté (63.04.01.47). Calm, nice atmosphere; regional cooking. ROOMS B–D. MEALS B–E. Shut Sunday evening, Monday.

MONTFLANQUIN

[LOT-ET-GARONNE]

Delightful 13th-century *bastide* built by the man who started these fortified villages for Edward III of England – Alphonse de Poitiers, Count of Toulouse and brother of King Louis IX of France. This one he built for the French. It stands on a steep hill overlooking the river Lède, a tributary of the Lot, 14km N of Villeneuve. The market square is absolutely delightful, retaining its arcades on all sides, and is still used for a weekly market with a lot of poultry for sale.

Narrow streets with timbered houses run into the square and the encircling road has superb views over the Lède and Lot rivers and even as far as Château de Biron in the Dordogne. The church, massively fortified, dominates the pleasant little town.

MARKETS Thursday: poultry; Saturday and Tuesday in summer: farm produce

FESTIVALS 24 June – Feux de St Jean; July – Music Festival, Lace Fair

MONSEMPRON – LIBOS

[LOT-ET-GARONNE]

3km W of Fumel on D911 dominating the right bank of the Lot, the little town has a fine Romanesque church with interesting features. 11km S by D102 is Tournon d'Agenais in a lovely hillside site. The surrounding countryside is planted with vines and maize, shaded by trees. There is another view southward from the little public gardens. It is an old *bastide*, but most of the arcades have gone from its main square. Houses have been built along the old walls.

MONTBRUN

[LOT]

Hamlet of sixty-one people in very attractive position rising in tiers on a projecting rock above the river Lot, surrounded by steep cliffs. It faces Saut de la Mounine (*see* Cajarc, page 72). Above it stand the ruins of the Cardaillac family castle of Montbrun.

HOTEL

La Ferme de Montbrun, on D662 (65.40.67.71). A restored farm in the country where they serve local dishes well cooked in generous quantities at reasonable prices. Very nice atmosphere. Only two rooms C. MEALS C–E. Shut Wednesday (except July–August); 1 November–Easter.

MONTCABRIER
[LOT]

Village to the north of Puy-l'Évêque, 5km above Duravel (page 88). It is on a beautiful stretch of road D673 which runs alongside the little Thèze river which joins the Lot just over the border in Lot-et-Garonne near the heavily industrialised town of Fumel. Montcabrier has an ancient church partly rebuilt in the 14th century, with a lovely Flamboyant doorway and attractive belfry. There are some old houses and ruins of a château-fort and of ancient churches.

HOTEL

Relais de la Dolce (65.36.53.42). Delicious 14th-century house in woodland. *Relais du Silence* offering '*calme, repos et tranquillité*'. ROOMS G. MEALS E–G. Open Easter–October.

MONTCUQ
[LOT]

At the end of the D653 road which heads SW off the N20 just S of Cahors, the village is on a hill overlooking the Petite Barguelonne river. The tall tower is all that remains of a castle and village fortifications. From here are wide views over the hills and valleys. There are photogenic old timber houses and two churches (one from the 14th century), with interesting wall paintings.

The D653 becomes D693 at Montcuq and leads in 12km to the old *bastide* town of Lauzerte in Tarn-et-Garonne. It is worth visiting. The country around it is called *Quercy Blanc* (White Quercy) though no longer in Lot.

TOURIST INFORMATION Mairie (15 June–15 September 65.22.94.04)

FESTIVALS July, August – Festival de Quercy Blanc. Early November – Horse-riding Endurance Championship during Les Deux Jours de Montcuq

HOTEL

Parc, at St Jean on road to Fumel (65.31.81.82). *Logis de France.* ROOMS B–C. MEALS A–F. Shut 30 October–15 March.

MONTECH
[TARN-ET-GARONNE]

Little town on D928 beside the Canal Latéral de la Garonne which takes boats to Toulouse, very near to Agre forest. It is 14km SW of Montauban and is a useful stopover place to avoid bigger towns.

MARKET Tuesday

HOTEL

Notre-Dame, place Jean-Jaurès (63.64.77.45). Entirely renovated. True traditional regional cooking. ROOMS B–C. MEALS A–E. Shut 1–15 November.

MONTPEZAT-DE-QUERCY
[TARN-ET-GARONNE]

Lovely old town on the N20 with covered arcades and old houses in timber and stone. It was the home of the Des Près family in the 14th to 15th centuries. Five of them became bishops. The first, Pierre, a Cardinal, built the Collegiate Church of St Martin in 1337, dedicated to St Martin of Tours. It is a simple, harmonious building, quite small with a single nave and no side-aisles. It is well worth seeing for the tapestries specially made to fit the sanctuary and given to the church by Jean Des Près, who was Bishop of Montauban when he died in 1539 at the age of twenty-two! The Des Près seem to have kept the job in the family. His tapestries are 25 metres long and 2 metres high, consisting of five panels divided into three sections. Richly coloured for their period, almost brilliant, they are in excellent condition. They show sixteen scenes in the life of St Martin, each with a quatrain in old French at the top of the panel.

St Martin was a Roman officer who became a Christian, split his military coat to give half to a shivering beggar and exchanged his war-horse for a donkey. He founded a monastery at Poitiers but was pulled out of it against his will to become Bishop of Tours. His fame as a miracle-worker brought crowds to Tours, and to avoid them he established the great teaching monastery at Marmoutier. It was he who jumped the Padirac chasm on a donkey to win a bet with the Devil to save a sackful of souls (page 54). The treasures of the church are interesting. They include three alabaster panels of the Nativity, Resurrection and Ascension brought from England. Cardinal Pierre Des Près has a statue and tomb carved in Carrara marble.

If you leave Montpezat to the west by D38 and turn left towards Montpezat station, another turn left takes you to a path beside a wood which leads to Saux church (4km). Once the centre of a thriving village, it now stands alone in the middle of a wood. Three dome bays are decorated with good 14th- to 15th-century frescoes, which include the legends of St George and St Catherine.

TOURIST INFORMATION Pavillon d'Accueil Touristique de Bas-Quercy (open high season – 63.02.05.65)

MONTRICOUX

[TARN-ET-GARONNE]

An old village built on terraces up the right bank of the Aveyron river 6km NW of Bruniquel. A square keep is all that remains of the 13th-century castle and part of the old perimeter walls still stand. Attractive medieval houses with timbering are in the old alleys. The river widens here in a fertile plain.

FESTIVAL July–August – Music Festival

HOTEL

Relais du Postillon, on D964 (63.67.23.58). ROOMS B–C. MEALS A–E. Shut Friday evening, Saturday lunch in winter; 20–30 November.

NÉRAC
[LOT-ET-GARONNE]

Very pleasant town astride the Baïse river, 30km W of Agen. You cross an old Gothic hump-bridge to reach the warren of little narrow streets called Petit-Nérac, the old town with the castle. Only one wing remains of the castle where the great Queen of Navarre, Marguerite d'Angoulême (1492–1549) reigned over a court which was brilliantly scholarly and so amusing. She was the sister of the flamboyant François I of France and after being widowed, married Henri d'Albret in 1527, titular King of Navarre. She encouraged the arts, learning and agriculture. She herself wrote poetry and the famous prose work *Heptameron*, an exploration of the meaning of human experience in the form of a series of conversational stories. She helped and sheltered religious reformers, encouraging Guillaume Briconnet in the reforms of his diocese of Meaux and sheltered the humanist Lefèvre and Marot the religious reformer.

She was mother of Jeanne d'Albret and the grandmother of Henri IV of France. Nérac was a base from which the Protestant armies of Navarre set out to fight the Catholics.

The arcaded Renaissance front gives an idea of the old castle. The long walk by the river, Promenade de la Garonne, is believed by some scholars to have been Shakespeare's setting in *Love's Labour Lost*: 'Navarre – a park with a palace in it'. It is now a public park with a fountain commemorating Marguerite and an equestrian statue of Henri. Fontaine de Fleurette, with the reclining figure of a girl beside a pool, is the memorial to a gardener's daughter who drowned herself in the pool after Henri seduced her and deserted her. Le Vert Galant was not so gallant, it seems, when he was young.

The newer part of the town on the left bank was built in the 19th century. Armand Fallières, French President from 1906–13, has a memorial on allées d'Albret. He was mayor of Nérac for many years. Another memorial is to Darlan, the French admiral who was called Minister of National Defence in the French wartime Vichy Government and who was Admiral in North Africa when the Vichy fleet was there. He expressed readiness to co-operate with the victorious Anglo-American Forces but was assassinated in 1942. He was born in Nérac in 1881.

The church, built in 1780, was designed by Victor Louis, architect of the Palais Royal in Paris.

TOURIST INFORMATION Pavillon des Bains (high season – 53.65.27.75); La Mairie (low season – 53.65.03.89)

MARKET Saturday

FESTIVALS May – Fête du Pays d'Albret; July–August – Music Festival; August – Painting Exhibition in Château.

HOTELS

D'Albret, 40 allées d'Albret (53.65.01.47). One of the best restaurants in the département to try local dishes at very reasonable prices. Cheapest weekday menu almost a giveaway. Hotel totally renovated. ROOMS B–E. MEALS A–E. Shut Monday in winter; September; 1–7 March.

Château, 7 av Mondenard (53.65.09.05). Town centre. Regional cooking; big choice of menus. ROOMS A–D. MEALS A–E. Shut October. Restaurant shut Sunday evening, Monday lunchtime from 1 November–30 June.

PENNE
[TARN-ET-GARONNE]

Of all the old hilltop villages of Tarn-et-Garonne this is probably the most spectacular. Overlooked by the ruins of its castle, it is perched on the side of a rocky spike rising sheer above the left bank of the Aveyron river.

The medieval castle above seems to be tumbling over the rock, ready to fall on to the flat roofs of the old houses.

To reach it you must walk along a narrow street lined with old houses, some with coats of arms. You pass round the church with a belfry in its tower and take a path to the ruins. It is too dangerous to go inside the ruins but they are well worth seeing from here, from the tip of the rock, from D133 S of Penne and from D33 north.

The castle played an important part in the Albigensian Crusade and later in the Hundred Years War, when it controlled much of the Aveyron valley and changed hands several times between the local troops and the English. The Lord of Penne supported the Albigensian Sect and fought bloody battles with Simon de Montfort, sent by Pope Julian III to wipe it out.

Do not mix up this Penne in Tarn-et-Garonne with Penne d'Agenais on the Lot river in Lot-et-Garonne (*see* below).

PENNE D'AGENAIS
[LOT-ET-GARONNE]

This village was a ruin in the 1950s, but now it is almost completely restored. Artists and artisans have moved in, and so have a lot of visitors.

10km E of Villeneuve-sur-Lot and on the left bank of the Lot river, it is an ancient stronghold which was long among the Aquitaine possessions of the English kings. Do not mix it up with the other Penne on the Aveyron in Tarn-et-Garonne (*see* above).

Place Gambetta is a pleasant shady terrace with a gateway Porte de Ville leading to old houses. The church Notre-Dame de Peyragude on top of the hill in Romanesque-Byzantine style is modern, but pilgrims still come in large numbers from May to June.

In the upper town are charming alleys with restored houses, decked with flowers in summer, some half-timbered with overhanging top storeys. The tourist office is in a very attractive house in place Paul-Froment. The Ricard gateway and fountain are named after Richard Lionheart of England who fortified the town. There are superb views over the Lot and Quercy countryside up here from a viewing table.

MARKET Sunday morning

FESTIVALS Fête week preceding 14th July; mid-July – Fair of Regional Produce La Tourtière (named after traditional tart); July–August – Exhibition of Artists and Artisans

HOTELS

Commerce et Restaurant Moulin, at Port de Penne, (53.41.21.34). Good value *Logis*. ROOMS B–C. MEALS A–C. Shut Sunday evening, Monday; September.

POUDENAS

[LOT-ET-GARONNE]

17km SW of Nérac, with château where Henri IV used to hunt (open mid-July–1 September afternoons). Lovely area. By the river Gélise and an old Roman bridge is a 14th-century mill, now an hotel (see below). Boat rides on the river from the hotel.

HOTEL

La Belle Gasconne, on D565 (53.65.71.58). Outstanding cooking in this converted mill owned by the mayor in a village of 309 people. His wife Marie-Claude Gracia does the cooking, best described as *Grande Régionale*, with local ingredients made into subtle dishes. Michelin star, plus a high 16–20 from Gault-Millau and accolades from my friend Marc Champérard, the great French gourmet-guide writer. 'She cooks like an angel with huge heart and incredible passion,' says Gault-Millau. And there is a cheap weekday menu, too. Fine collection of wines from south-west France. Romantic bedrooms (only six – so book ahead). ROOMS G. MEALS C–F. Shut Sunday evening, Monday except July, August; 1–15 January; 1–15 December.

PRAYSSAC

[LOT]

Pleasant little wine town with holiday amenities near the river Lot 10km E of Puy-l'Évêque. Some old houses. On D67, 3km towards the river is Clos de Gamot, where you can taste the superb red Cahors wine of Jean Jouffreau, made from grapes of one hundred-year-old vines.

HOTEL

Vidal, 3 rue des Garabets (65.22.41.78). Popular for years. ROOMS B–D. MEALS A–D. Shut Monday in winter; 8–31 January.

PUYLAROQUE
[TARN-ET-GARONNE]

The men who planned the medieval *bastides* put them on top of hills for defence and to give them long views over the countryside so that they had time to call in field workers behind fortified walls at the approach of any suspicious band. What a joy those views are to modern travellers!

From the esplanades of this Bas-Quercy *bastide* 14km NE of Caussade are wonderful views of the valleys of the little Candé and Lère rivers, the rolling Quercy countryside and to the Caussade and Montauban plains. The view from the esplanade near the church is especially fine.

There are tightly packed groups of nearly flat-roofed old houses in the narrow streets, and the church still has a massive, square belfry built as a watch-tower and a last line of defence. Poor Puylaroque was another village sacked in 1209 by De Montfort in his 'holy' crusade to wipe out the 'heretical' Albigensian Sect. He used it as an excuse to pillage, loot and destroy almost any village, manor or castle which stood in his path.

PUY L'ÉVÊQUE
[LOT]

Delightful little town by the Lot with golden-stone houses rising in tiers to the 14th-century church, town hall and inn.

From the esplanade are some of the finest views of the Lot

snaking away towards Cahors, and of the attractive, modern small suspension bridge which crosses to the new part of Puy l'Évêque – playing grounds and a few houses and holiday homes. The views from the terraces of the inn, the Bellevue, are almost as good – *Bellevue* indeed. All that is left of the Bishop of Cahors' castle is the 12th-century keep. The huge belfry porch of the church is flanked by a turret and buttresses. It was part of the town's defences. There is another fine view of the town from the opposite side of the suspension bridge.

HOTELS

Bellevue, place de la Truffière (65.21.30.70). Looks rather dull from the road and the front bar used by locals is bare. But views from terrace, dining room and some bedrooms are superb. Good value meals of old regional dishes. ROOMS B–C. MEALS A–E. Shut Sunday evening, Monday except 1 June–15 September; 15 November–1 March.

La Truffière, rue des Scafignous à la Truffière (65.21.34.54). ROOMS B–C. MEALS A–C. Restaurant shut Monday from 1 October–30 March.

PUJOLS

[*See* Villeneuve-sur-Lot, page 142]

PUYMIROL

[LOT-ET-GARONNE]

A fine *bastide* of 1246 on a hill over the Séoune valley, 16km E of Agen. It has a 13th-century church, arcaded square and some fine old houses, including l'Aubergade, 13th-century house which belonged to the Counts of Toulouse, now a superb restaurant (see below). The surrounding roads are attractive.

RESTAURANT

L'Aubergade, 52 rue Royale (53.95.31.46). Remarkable in an off-track village in a ravishing old house to find one of the greatest chefs in France. Still more remarkable that although Michel Trama does invent a few delicious dishes to please his modernistic clients he relies mostly on regional south-west cuisine with no frills, superbly executed. There were plans for an hotel in 1989. A splendid idea – I don't want to drive away after his meals. Very expensive – but normal for two Michelin stars, 19 out of 20 from Gault-Millau, top rating from Champérard and Relais Gourmand rating from Relais et Châteaux Hotels. MEALS G. Shut Monday except in June, July, August.

RIGNAC
[LOT]

Very photogenic village which would make a wonderful film set for a story of centuries past. Even the farms seem to be period pieces. Just off little D36 road 4.5km E of Rocamadour, 4.5km NW of Gramat. The imposing Château de Roumégouse, just off N140, has become a delightful Relais et Châteaux Hotel, serving superb food. It is a gorgeous neo-Gothic 'fairytale' château with pointed tower and fine views of the Causse de Gramat. One owner in the 1890s bribed the locals to rebuild their village out of sight of the castle, which shows that Rignac's 'other centuries' appearance is something of an illusion. The castle was used in the Second World War by the Resistance, then after the war, owned by de Gaulle's Paris hairdresser. Lucé Lainé, who runs it now with her husband Jean-Louis, used to run a Paris boutique for Maison de Marie Claire.

HOTEL

Château de Roumégouse (65.33.63.81). Absolutely charming with elegant service, the best regional cooking with a light touch, and just a touch of pleasant eccentricity. Superb terrace, luxurious bedrooms. Beautiful breakfasts. ROOMS E–G. MEALS D–G. Shut Tuesday (except evenings in July, August); early November–Easter.

RUDELLE

[LOT]

Old village on N140, 14km SE of Gramat, with a magnificent example of a medieval fortified church in which the villagers could make a last stand when attacked by enemies or marauding bands. It looks more like a fortress than a church. It was built in the 13th century by Bertrand de Cardaillac, Lord of Lacapelle-Marival. The ground floor, a vaulted hall, is still the parish church. A wooden staircase takes you up to the gallery. Then there is a trap door reached by a ladder which could be pulled up after you, and a stone staircase leading to an upper storey, lit by little slits through which arrows could be fired. This room is now used as a belfry. Another ladder and stone staircase leads to a second refuge, the terrace. The watchpath is machiolated for defence. From it you can see the whole village, where there is an old market hall.

ST ANTONIN-NOBLE-VAL

[TARN-ET-GARONNE]

This ancient Gallo-Roman resort was given the name *Noble-Val* because of its glorious setting. It rises above the right bank of the Aveyron river on the borders of Quercy and Rouergue, with vertical cliff rocks called Rochers d'Anglars on the opposite side of the valley.

The town grew around an 8th-century abbey and became prosperous in the Middle Ages. Old nearly flat-roofed houses of merchants from the 13th, 14th and 15th centuries line the streets of the old quarter around the old town hall and alleys wind down to the river. It is a most pleasant little town and a delightful centre for discovering the upper Aveyron valley and the gorges.

The former town hall is one of the oldest houses in France. It was built in 1125 for a landowner. By the 14th century it was the consul's residence. It was restored last century by Viollet-le-Duc, who restored Notre-Dame in Paris, much of Laon and the medieval fortified city of Carcassonne. It has two storeys. The first has a gallery of columns with skilfully carved statues of Adam and Eve and King Solomon. A tall, square tower is battlemented at the top. There is a museum of prehistory and local folklore inside.

The river here is popular with canoeists.

Three kms along D75 NE is Grotte du Bosc, with 200 metre galleries of a dried-up river going 200 metres beneath the Aveyron plateau. Stalactites hang from the roof. There is a small museum of prehistory (shut mid-September–31 May). Continue along D75, then take D20 right and D33 left and you find the former abbey of Beaulieu-en-Rouergue in a lovely setting in the Seye valley. It was founded in 1144 but the fine abbey church which remains was built in the 13th century. You can see also the old chapterhouse and a Gothic storeroom, with an art gallery in the dormitory above (open Palm Sunday–30 September, except Tuesday).

Roads from St Antonin along the Aveyron river are delightful. Eastward the D958 and D20 lead to the charming villages of Verfeil (page 140) and Varen (page 139). Westward the best road is D115, then the little D115B on the left bank, crossing to Cazals and following this little corniche road to the Gorges d'Aveyron. St Antonin is a delightful town which looks a little as if it slipped from the Midi.

MARKET Sunday morning

FESTIVALS Musical Soirées mid-July–mid-August

HOTEL

Viollet-le-Duc, place Marché (63.68.21.00). The conversion in 1987 of this fine very old house into a comfortable hotel is a great blessing. It is charming, with elegant rooms, well equipped, open every day all the year, and with a very wide choice of menus in restaurant and grill. ROOMS C–D. MEALS A–F.

RESTAURANT

La Bergerie (63.30.60.58). A pity that this farm restaurant's opening times are so seasonal, for the farm-style cooking with ample portions is delicious and the price, which includes a simple wine of Tarn, is very reasonable indeed. MEALS D (all in).

Open lunch and dinner July, August except for Monday evening, Tuesday. Rest of year lunch only. Closed Tuesday.

ST MARTIN DE VERS

[LOT]

On the little D32 road south of Labastide-Murat. A picturesque village with old peasant houses almost perfectly preserved. Fine old church.

ST MAURIN

[LOT-ET-GARONNE]

A rather strange old village built among ruins of an 11th-century Benedictine abbey. Old houses with round tiles and towers, including a fortified, towered mairie. It has an old market hall, too, and the old abbey church, restored in the 17th century. St Maurin is 8½km E of Puymirol on the attractive D16.

ST PIERRE-TOIRAC

[Lot]

Another remarkable fortified church in a little village on the right bank of the Lot very near to Larroque-Toirac (page 102). Built between the 11th and 14th centuries, it was a Benedictine church fortified in the 15th century. The village is one of many attractive villages along this river bank.

ST SULPICE

[Lot]

The Hébrard family of St Sulpice were so powerful in the Middle Ages that it ruled most of the Célé valley and beyond and the area was called the *Hébrardie*. The Lords of Hébrard set up priories and were powerful enough to protect their people even in the wild times of the Hundred Years War. They were soldiers, rulers and churchmen. One was Bishop of Cahors, another Bishop of Coïmbra, the powerful church region of Portugal. The 12th-century castle, rebuilt in the 14th to 15th centuries, still belongs to the family. Some of the 13th-century ramparts are still there. The village itself lies under an overhanging cliff.

SAULIAC

[Lot]

Another Célé valley village, 9km upstream from Cabrerets and with an attractive road D24 joining it to the Lot 10km away. Sauliac is an old village pinned against a fearsome cliff of coloured rock. It has a 13th- to 15th-century château, the ruins of Château Sauliac, and fortified caves used by the local peasants as a refuge in wars. They are way up the cliff. The most agile climbed up on ropes or ladders. The aged, the sick and animals were hoisted up in baskets by rope. It must have been a terrible life for peasants in the Hundred Years War when gangs of pillaging soldiers of both sides roamed the countryside stealing crops, farm animals, looting houses, killing men and raping women.

SAUX
[Lot]

In the very SW corner of Lot, S of Puy-l'Évêque among little roads S of D656. Several château-manor houses around here, including Château d'Ays, altered over four centuries (15th to 18th). The church, once a village centre, is isolated in woods. The three domed bays are painted with excellent 14th- to 15th-century frescoes with stories of the life of Jesus, the story of St Catherine and the legend of St George.

SEPTFONDS
[Tarn-et-Garonne]

Bastide on D926, 7km NE of Caussade, built in 1271.

RESTAURANT

Saint-Mamet, 43 cours Sadi-Carnot (63.64.97.11). Remarkable value, with good, rather rich dishes and rustic atmosphere, away from the main road, and country views. Meals B–C. Shut Tuesday evening, Wednesday lunch; February.

SOULOMÈS
[Lot]

Only 3km SE of Labastide-Murat on D17. Superb views from 2km S over this hilly countryside. In the chancel of the Gothic church, interesting 14th-century wall paintings have been uncovered, showing scenes in the life of Christ, including one of Christ resurrected before the eyes of a Knight of St John of Malta and another showing St Thomas doubting.

SOUSCEYRAC
[Lot]

From St Céré a lovely road D673 runs 16km E to Sousceyrac. Forests begin here and there's a lake called Lac de Luzetta. Just to the north is the Château de Grugnac.

HOTEL

Au Déjeuner de Sousceyrac (65.33.00.56). Rooms B–C. Meals B–E. Shut Monday low season; 3 January–mid-March.

THÉGRA
[Lot]

Village known for an interesting old church (13th-century crypt), strongly fortified manor house from 1450 which was 'modernised' to make it more habitable in the 17th century, and the historic carnival through the streets on the third Sunday in August. It lies on the tiny D11, 6km from Gramat by D677, turning left at Lavergne, where there is a good restaurant.

RESTAURANT

Le Limargue (at Lavergne, see above 65.38.76.02). Meals B–E. Shut Wednesday off-season; 15–31 January; 15–31 October.

TONNEINS
[Lot-et-Garonne]

Town on the Garonne with good river views, where D911 meets N113. Canoeing centre, and holds an annual veteran car rally the first weekend in September.

TOURIST INFORMATION Syndicat d'Initiative, boul Charles de Gaulle (53.79.22.79)
MARKETS Saturday mornings; Wednesday
FESTIVALS July – Lace Fair; May – Exhibition of Old Cars; September (1st weekend) – Old Car Rally; Exhibition of Paintings and Crafts

HOTEL

Castel Ferron, route Marmande (53.84.59.99). In an 18th-century château, beautifully furnished. Park, swimming pool, horse-riding; quiet and restful. ROOMS E–F. MEALS C–F

TOURNON D'AGENAIS

[LOT-ET-GARONNE]

6km S of Monsempron-Libros. Hilltop village with superb views over Lot valley.

FESTIVALS 15 August: Fête des Rosiéres (Innocent Maidens)

TOUZAC

[LOT]

A charming village on the Lot downriver from Puy-l'Évêque hardly mentioned by French guides, though there is also a useful bridge here for those wanting to leave D911 and cross into the little roads of the wine country south of the river. The great actress Marguerite Moreno had a house and was buried here. Any mention it does get is for its 14th-century mill which is now a delightful hotel Moulin de la Source Bleue. It has a charming, rustic dining-room with open fireplace. In fact, it is three old mills with paths, lawns, trees and steps right down to the river. The writer Colette used to come here regularly when visiting her friend Marguerite Moreno.

HOTEL

Source Bleue (65.36.52.01). Member of the delightful *Moulin Etape* club of good French hotels in old mills, all of them splendid. ROOMS C–F. MEALS C–E. Shut 19 March–30 October; restaurant shut Tuesdays

VAILLLAC
[LOT]

5km E of the N20 and 5km NW of Labastide-Murat by the little D17, it has a huge, strong feudal castle built around 1470. Unfortunately it is not open to the public. Splendid stables.

VAISSAC
[TARN-ET-GARONNE]

Village on the little Longues Aigues river south of D115 between Montauban and Bruniquel among hills and woods. Quiet area not visited by tourists.

HOTEL

Terrassier (63.30.94.60). Family-run *Logis de France* with home-made *confits* and other conserves and local ingredients. ROOMS B–C. MEALS A–F. Restaurant shut Friday evening.

VALENCE d'AGEN
[TARN-ET-GARONNE]

A busy little town on the Tarn river in Tarn-et-Garonne but only 26km SE of Agen where N113 meets D953. The remains of a *bastide* of 1279 include three sides of its main square with old houses in the side streets. There is a nuclear station 3km downstream at Golfech (guided visits).

TOURIST INFORMATION Syndicat d'Initiative (63.39.61.67)

MARKET Tuesday – including Truffles and *Foie Gras* in

December and January (*Marché au gras*). Chicken Fair (*Concours de Volailes*) 3rd Tuesday in December; Foie Gras Concours (*Concours de Gras*) 3rd Tuesday in January. Gosling Fair (*Concours aux Oisons*) 3rd Tuesday in February

HOTELS

Tout Va Bien, 35 rue République (63.39.54.83). Completely renovated. Nice situation, quiet hotel. Experienced chef; traditional Quercy dishes. Country views. ROOMS B–D. MEALS B–E. Shut January. Restaurant shut Monday.

France (63.39.63.31). *Logis de France*. ROOMS A–D. MEALS A–E. Shut Saturday; December.

RESTAURANT

La Campagnette, 2km on route Cahors D953 (63.39.65.97). Charming country restaurant with flower garden and subdued décor. The cooking is interesting and very good. Mostly light and inventive but some good regional dishes included. Good choice of succulent desserts. Good cheaper menus as well as a good carte. MEALS B–F. Shut Sunday evening; Monday except July–August; 22–27 May; 4–9 September.

VAREN
[TARN-ET-GARONNE]

A splendid old market town on the right bank of the Aveyron, 16km east of St Antonin-Noble-Val, Varen was once a highly fortified town. You still enter the old part of the town through a fortified doorway, Porte El Faoure, which leads to delightful narrow streets lined by houses with timberwork, overhanging upper storeys and flat roofs of round tiles.

The strong keep of the old castle has a battlemented watch-path and protruding turret. Here the Prior of Varen, Lord of the town, shut himself up when he refused to accept the decisions of his superior, the Bishop of Rodez. He declared independence. The bishop had the monks removed from his priory and replaced.

The 11th-century Romanesque church was originally built into the town's defensive wall. A doorway was opened in 1802.

VAYRAC
[LOT]

Village 10km E of Martel on D703, very near the Dordogne. The plateau falls away in steep cliffs at its borders with streams flowing into the Dordogne below. The highest point of the plateau is Puy d'Issolud (311 metres) reached by a little road westward from Vayrac.

In the time of the Gauls, Puy d'Issolud was surrounded by solid earth and dry stone defences. It was one of the really strong Gaulish towns, the most likely site of Uxellodunum, place of the last stand of the Gauls against Julius Caesar. The battle was fierce and cruel and after a stream had been diverted by the Romans through underground caverns in which the Gauls were sheltering, the Romans won. Caesar was so furious at the Gaulish resistance that he ordered the right hands of all the prisoners to be cut off. That was typical of Caesar's cruelty. Another tribe in what is now France put up such a good fight that he had the whole tribe killed.

From the plateau are views of the Dordogne.

VERFEIL
[TARN-ET-GARONNE]

A truly charming village on the river Seye, north of Varen on the D20, it has a stone covered market surrounded by old houses, flower-decked in summer. A 17th-century statue of Christ in the church came from the former Abbey of Beaulieu-en-Rouergue to the north-west.

VERS
[Lot]

On D653, the attractive road which hugs the right bank of the Lot eastward from Cahors. The Vers river joins the Lot here and the road follows the Vers. Vers' Chapelle de Notre-Dame-de-Velles (11th to 12th centuries) is an ancient pilgrimage chapel of Lot sailors.

HOTEL

Chalets (65.31.40.83). Rooms B–C. Meals A–D.

VIANNE
[Lot-et-Garonne]

Bastide of 1284 which had become almost abandoned until a glassworks opened there in recent years. On the Baïse river 9km N of Nèrac, it is on D642, 6km S of the A62 Motorway. Its fortified walls are intact, as are its four gateways and Romanesque church with an old fortified belltower.

VILLEBRUMIER – VILLEMUR
[Tarn-et-Garonne]

An old *bastide* on the Tarn, 16km S of Montauban by D21. This is in the lower valley of the Tarn with wide valleys of rich soil where many crops grow – wheat and maize, early vegetables, fruit and vines.

Beyond Villebrumier, coming from Montauban, the hills rise gently to Villemur-sur-Tarn, just over the Haute-Garonne border. Another old fortified town in which the Vieux-Moulin Saracen tower remains.

VILLENEUVE-SUR-LOT

[LOT-ET-GARONNE]

A large and very strong *bastide* built in 1253 by Alphonse de Poitiers, Count of Toulouse and brother of Louis IX of France (St Louis), who built most of the early *bastides* for Edward III of England. This one was built for Louis but was soon taken by the English, who in the 13th century built a bridge with uneven arches which is still there, with a chapel right by the water called 'Our Lady at the end of the Bridge'. The Lot flows right through the town, held by retaining walls.

Two stone and brick gates of the old ramparts remain, Porte de Paris, and the three-storeyed Porte de Pujols with mullioned windows. Both are topped with fortifications. Old houses, towers and tiny streets are around the town but the past few years have brought many buildings and much more traffic, for it is a business centre and important market for fruit and early vegetables from the rich valley, especially plums. It is still very pleasant.

The brick church of St Catherine, built in Romanesque-Byzantine style, was in fact not consecrated until 1937, though it contains restored 14th- to 15th-century stained glass from an earlier church and 17th to 18th-century gilded wooden statues.

The municipal museum (Gaston Rapin Museum) is on the corner of rue Voltaire, near Porte de Pujols. It includes an interesting Musée de la Prune (Plum Museum), showing a history of growing methods and tools.

From Porte de Pujols, an old Roman road offers a 3km walk to the delightful old hilltop walled village of Pujols. Enter beneath the belfry tower of 13th-century St Nicolas church and you are immediately among old houses packed inside 13th-century ramparts. The valley still has many timbered houses with porch roofs and charming Renaissance houses. In a modern block is the best known restaurant in the area – La Toque Blanche where Bernard Lebrun makes use of the lovely fresh vegetables from Villeneuve market to cook old-style regional dishes with old-fashioned sauces.

TOURIST INFORMATION Tourist Office behind theatre (53.70.31.35)

MARKET Tuesday and Saturday.

FESTIVAL (Pujols): July, August – Arts and Crafts Exhibition

HOTELS

Chênes, at Pujols (53.49.04.55). Modern, air-conditioned hotel. Toque Blanche restaurant. ROOMS C–E. Open all year.
Parc, 13 boul. de la Marine (53.70.01.68). Mapotel. Big enclosed terrace overlooking garden. ROOMS D–E. MEALS B–E. Shut Sunday evening, Monday lunch.

RESTAURANTS

Toque Blanche, Pujols (53.49.00.30). *See above.* MEALS C–F. Shut Sunday evening, Monday; 26 June–10 July; 27 November–4 December; part February.
Hostellerie du Rooy, chemin de Labourdette D661 (53.70.48.48). Best restaurant in Villeneuve itself. In quiet, pretty grounds with old trees. MEALS C–F. Shut Sunday evening, Wednesday; 15 February–1 March.

VILLERÉAL
[LOT-ET-GARONNE]

In the NE corner of Lot-et-Garonne, almost in Périgord and not far from Biron castle, Villeréal is yet another *bastide* built by Louis IX's brother, Alphonse de Poitiers, to keep out the English and which the English soon captured. There are still the old arcades down two sides of the main square. These are called *cornières* in this area. The market hall, supported by oak pillars, was built in the 14th century with 16th- to 17th-century upper storey. Many of the old houses have overhanging storeys. The 13th-century church is fortified with two towers. It is an attractive old town which does not look like a museum. There is a lake below the town.

TOURIST INFORMATION Mairie (53.36.00.37)
MARKET Saturday; 1st and 3rd Monday of each month

HOTEL

Du Lac, route de Bergerac (53.36.01.39). Holiday-tourist hotel shut in winter. In country setting, swimming pool, fishing. Good choice of menus. ROOMS B–D. MEALS A–D. Shut mid-October–mid-April. Restaurant shut Monday lunch, Saturday lunch.

VIRE
[LOT]

On the Cahors Wine Route among many vineyards on the left bank of the Lot, 3km from Puy-l'Évêque. A port on the opposite bank left over from the days when wine was carried by boat down-river. Great *Fêtes des Vins de Cahors* at the end of July.

XAINTRAILLES
[LOT-ET-GARONNE]

Magnificent views from this isolated hilltop hamlet 11km NW of Nérac. You can see right over the motorway to the Garonne and southward for miles over Landes forests. The château, built in the 12th century, was reconstructed in the 15th century by one of Joan of Arc's companions Jean Poton de Xaintrailles. It is privately owned but visits can sometimes be arranged by phone (53.65.51.49).

MAPS

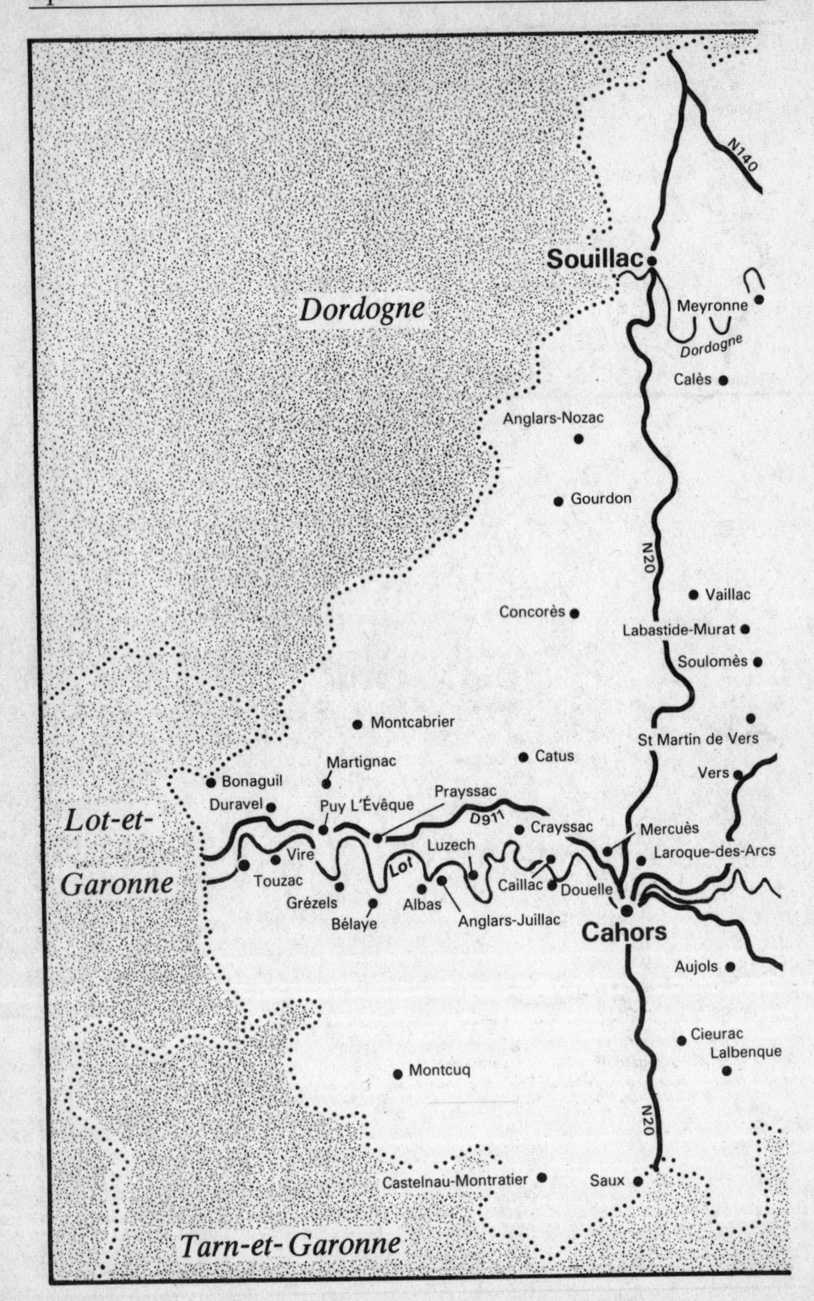

Souillac
N140
Dordogne
Meyronne
Dordogne
Calès
Anglars-Nozac
Gourdon
N20
Vaillac
Concorès
Labastide-Murat
Soulomès
Montcabrier
St Martin de Vers
Catus
Martignac
Vers
Bonaguil
Prayssac
Duravel
Puy L'Évêque
D911
Lot-et-
Garonne
Crayssac
Mercuès
Luzech
Vire
Laroque-des-Arcs
Lot
Touzac
Caillac
Douelle
Grézels
Albas
Bélaye
Anglars-Juillac
Cahors
Aujols
Cieurac
Lalbenque
Montcuq
N20
Castelnau-Montratier
Saux
Tarn-et-Garonne

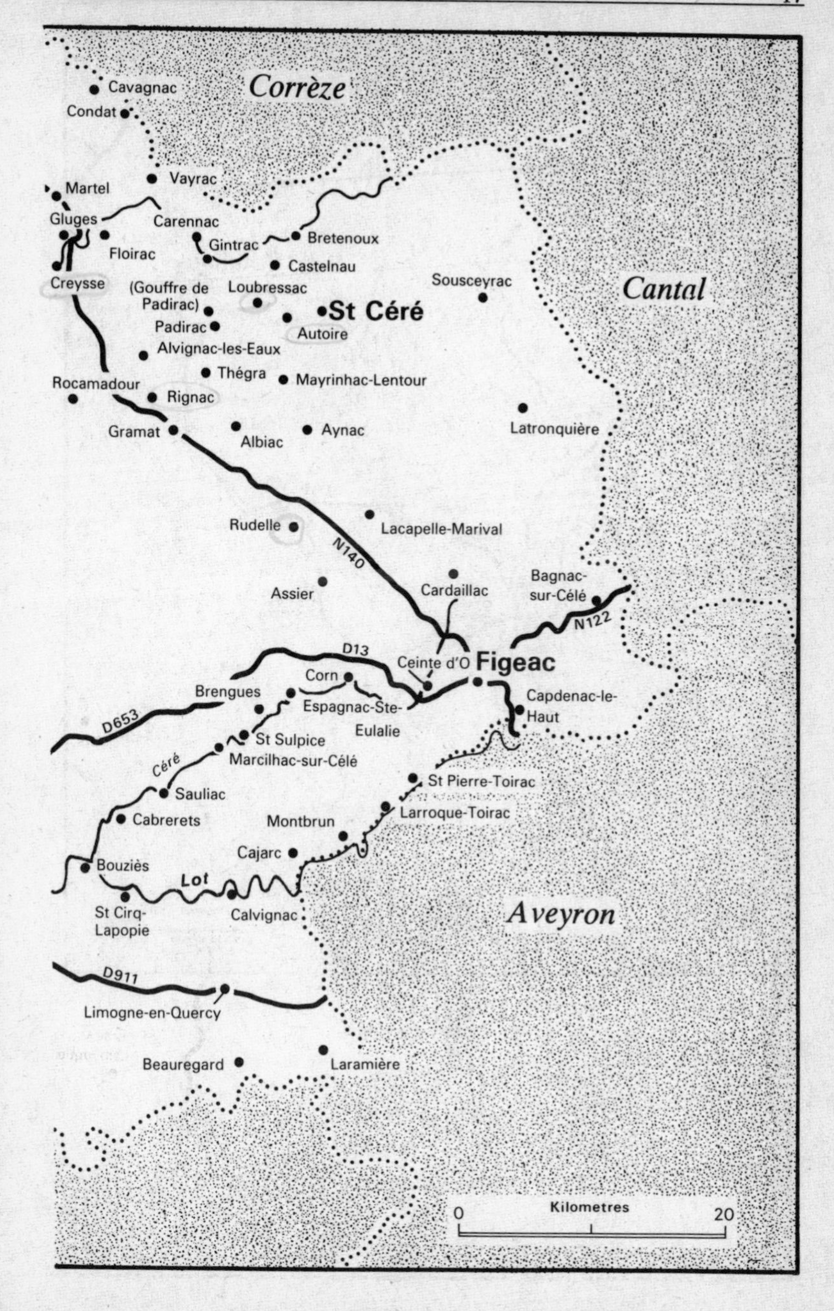
Corrèze
Cavagnac
Condat
Vayrac
Martel
Gluges
Carennac
Floirac
Gintrac
Bretenoux
Castelnau
Creysse
(Gouffre de Padirac)
Loubressac
Sousceyrac
Cantal
St Céré
Padirac
Autoire
Alvignac-les-Eaux
Thégra
Mayrinhac-Lentour
Rocamadour
Rignac
Gramat
Albiac
Aynac
Latronquière
Rudelle
Lacapelle-Marival
N140
Assier
Cardaillac
Bagnac-sur-Célé
N122
D13
Ceinte d'O
Figeac
Corn
Brengues
Espagnac-Ste-Eulalie
Capdenac-le-Haut
D653
St Sulpice
Marcilhac-sur-Célé
Célé
Sauliac
St Pierre-Toirac
Cabrerets
Larroque-Toirac
Montbrun
Cajarc
Bouziès
Lot
St Cirq-Lapopie
Calvignac
Aveyron
D911
Limogne-en-Quercy
Beauregard
Laramière
Kilometres
0
20

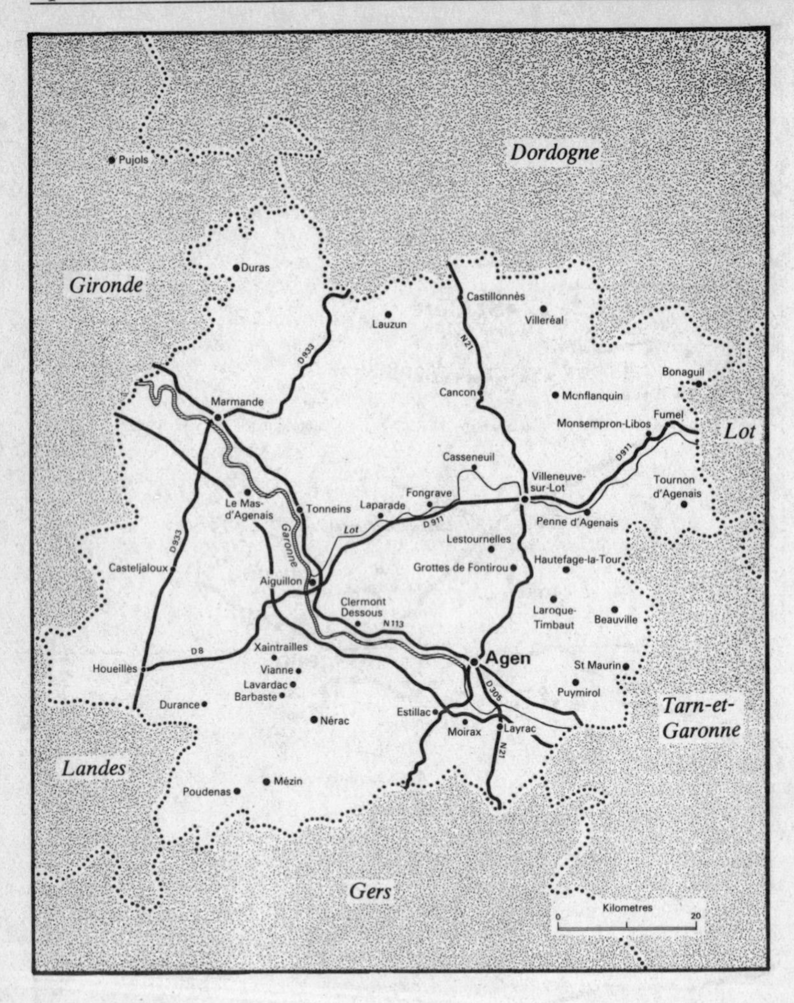

3 *Lot-et-Garonne*

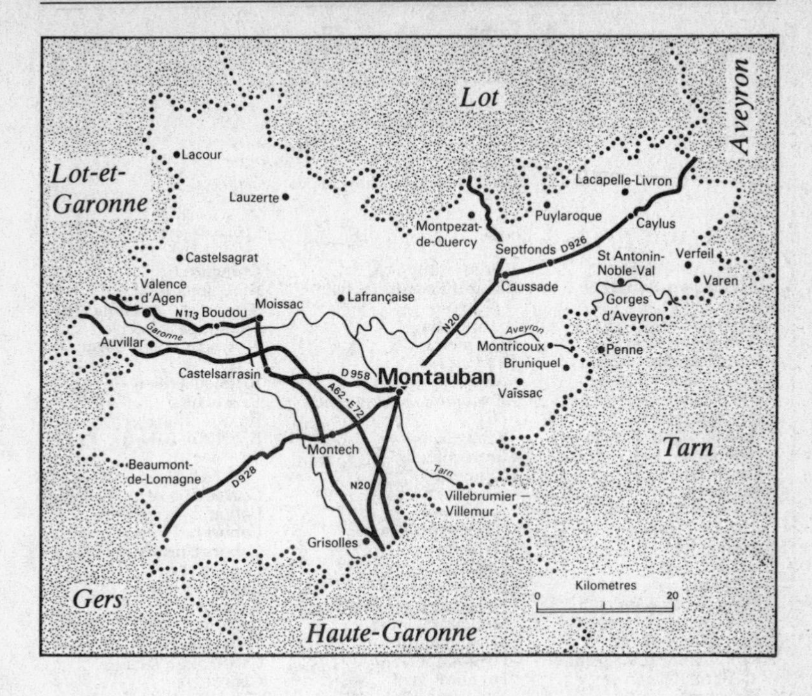

4 *Tarn-et-Garonne*

INDEX

Names of hotels and restaurants appear in *italics*.

Index compiled by Peva Keane